W9-BSC-798

The Complete Writings of Alexander Mack

Edited by
William R. Eberly

BMH Books
P.O. Box 544
Winona Lake, IN 46590

Explanation of Logo

The logo used on the title pages of the volumes of this series is derived from a seal which has been attributed to Alexander Mack, Jr. (1712-1803), son of the first Brethren minister and himself an active elder in colonial America. The *Brethren Encyclopedia* article on this "Mack seal" states, referring to the religious symbols: "Central to these is the cross, on which is superimposed a heart, suggesting a strong emphasis on sacrifice and devotion. The importance of bearing spiritual fruit is represented graphically by a vine, laden with grapes, whose branches spring from the heart. All of these symbols express an understanding of discipleship that was significant in the early history of the Brethren" (p. 775). The "Mack seal" has often been used by Brethren congregations on stationery, artwork, and publications.

ISBN 0-936693-12-6

Copyright 1991
BMH Books
Winona Lake, Indiana

Printed in U.S.A.

Contents

Eberhard Ludwig Grubers
Grundforschende

Fragen,

welche denen

neuen Täufern

im Witgensteinischen, insonder-
heit zu beantworten vorgelegt waren,
sammt:

beygefügten kurzen und einfältigen Ant-
worten auf dieselben, vormals schriftlich
heraus gegeben von einem

Aufrichtigen Mitglied

der Gemeinde zu Witgenstein,

und nun auf vieles Verlangen,

zum öffentlichen Druck befördert.

Zweyte Auflage.

Germantown,

gedruckt und zu finden bey Christoph Saur,
I 7 7 4.

Second edition of *Basic Questions* by
Alexander Mack. Published by Christopher
Saur in 1774 in Germantown (Philadelphia),
Pennsylvania.

Preface

The writings of the founders of religious movements are held in great esteem by the members of those movements. For those who are members of the Brethren movement, the writings of Alexander Mack are especially significant. In earlier times, some of these writings have been more accessable than now. It has been many decades since these materials have been available in an inexpensive publication containing only these selected writings.

A great number of religious movements incorporate the word "Brethren" in their names. The somewhat formal beginning of the "Mack" Brethren movement was in the small German village of Schwarzenau in 1708. By about 1735 many members had emigrated to North America and the remaining members in Europe had merged into other denominations. In America, several divisions split the church. Today the following denominations represent the Schwarzenau Brethren Movement in the United States: The Brethren Church; Church of the Brethren; Dunkard Brethren; Grace Brethren Church; and Old German Baptist Brethren Church. Several independent church bodies outside the United States represent churches established by the American Brethren bodies.

Almost all of the pieces in this book first appeared in Germany between 1708 and 1720. Most of the translations are by Donald Durnbaugh which appeared in his books *European Origins of the Brethren* (Elgin, 1958) and *The Brethren in Colonial America* (Elgin, 1967). We are grateful to Dr. Durnbaugh and to the Brethren Press for permission to use material from these volumes. The translation of Mack's hymn, Count the Cost, by Ora Garber is also by permission of the Brethren Press. Hedda Durnbaugh's translation of the same hymn appeared in her book, *The German Hymnody of the Brethren* (1986), published by the Brethren Encyclopedia, Inc.

With the inclusion of the fragments written in the Mack Bible, we believe this volume includes all known writings from the pen of Alexander Mack. One cannot fully understand and appreciate the Brethren movement without carefully reading the words of its founder and first minister.

William R. Eberly, editor
Manchester College
North Manchester, Indiana

v

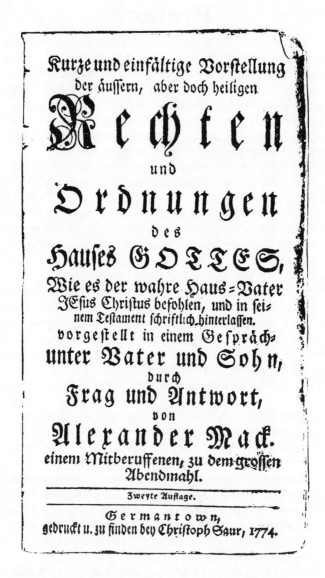

Kurze und einfältige Vorstellung
der äussern, aber doch heiligen

Rechten

und

Ordnungen

des

Hauses GOTTES,

Wie es der wahre Haus=Vater
JEsus Christus befohlen, und in sei=
nem Testament schriftlich hinterlassen.
vorgestellt in einem Gespräch=
unter Vater und Sohn,
durch
Frag und Antwort,
von
Alexander Mack.
einem Mitberuffenen, zu dem grossen
Abendmahl.

Zweyte Auflage.

Germantown,
gedruckt u. zu finden bey Christoph Saur, 1774.

Second edition of *Rights and Ordinances* by
Alexander Mack. Published by Christopher
Saur in 1744 in Germantown (Philadelphia),
Pennsylvania.

The Life of
Alexander Mack

Mack, Alexander, 1679-1735, the first minister and organizer of the first Brethren (New Baptist or *Neue Taufer*) in 1708. Born in Schriesheim in the Palatinate, Mack was the son of Johann Philipp and Christina Fillbrun Mack. He was baptized on July 27, 1679, by Ludwig Agricola, pastor of the local Reformed Church, and christened Alexander in honor of his uncle Alexander Fillbrun, postmaster of the neighboring village of Neckarhausen. Mack attended school in the local church during the War of the Grand Alliance with France (1689-97), but his education was interrupted several times when the Mack family had to flee to the hills for safety. As a youth, Mack also worked in the family mill and vineyards. Evidence suggests that Alexander was intended for an education at Heidelberg U., while his two older brothers would inherit the family milling business. However, when the oldest brother died in 1689, it was decided that Alexander should become a miller. The Mack family had been prominent in Schriesheim's religious institutions since 1560, and Mack's father had twice served as mayor of Schriesheim. Alexander was expected to continue in this tradition.

On Jan. 18, 1701, he married Anna Margarethe Kling, from a prominent Schriesheim family. While living in Schriesheim, their sons Johann Valentin and Johannes, were born. Mack and his wife soon became involved with Pietism. About 1705, they became devoted followers of Ernst Christoph Hochmann von Hochenau, a Radical Pietist and noted Separatist. Mack began holding illegal Bible study and prayer services in his home. In order to devote more time

1

to his religious activities, in March, 1706, he sold his interest in the family mill to his older brother. This was a disappointment to his father, who died shortly thereafter.

During the summer of 1706, Mack traveled with Hockmann in the Marienborn area, northeast of Frankfurt/Main, preaching and teaching in pietistic groups there. Mack invited Hochmann to conduct a similar mission in Schriesheim. In August Hochmann arrived in Schriesheim with several companions. They held services in Mack's home, preached in the streets, and distributed literature to the village citizens. The success of this mission, with its joyful contagiousness, caused the Reformed Church council, or consistory, at Heidelberg to petition the government to stop "this evil before it spreads further." On the evening of August 22, while Hochmann was leading a service in Mack's home, Heidelberg's chief law enforcement officer appeared and dispersed the meeting. That same evening, Mack and his wife gathered together the possessions they could carry and fled from Schriesheim, finding their way eventually to Schwarzenau in Wittgenstein, a tolerant principality widely know as a refuge for religious dissidents.

During the spring and summer of 1707, Mack and Hochmann traveled together on preaching missons to bring encouragement to Pietists living in other areas. Alexander Mack, Jr., later wrote that his father also "visited in heartfelt love, from time to time, various meetings of the Mennonites in Germany." During the autumn of 1707, Mack and Hochmann separated, with Mack returning to his family at Schwarzenau. Hochmann continued on to Nurnberg, where he was arrested and imprisoned for more than a year. The intensity of their commitment and love for each other led the group which formed around Mack at Schwarzenau to develop a functioning, though not formally organized, mutual aid society. Mack, who was probably the wealthiest of all the refugees, shared his wealth generously with those in need.

A question much discussed in peitistic gatherings in Schwarzenau was the rite of baptism. For Mack, the New Testament clearly indicated that adult baptism was a necessary initiation into the body of Christ. Two "foreign brethren," probably Dutch Collegiants, who visited Schwarzenau in the summer of 1708, strongly urged that the Mack group begin to practice adult baptism in spite of its illegality. Encouraged by these two visitors, Mack and another member of the group composed a letter asking the imprisoned Hochmann for his counsel concerning such a step. Hochmann replied immmediately, expressing no opposition, providing baptism followed true repentance and faith. He cautioned them, however, to "count the cost" and avoid a sectarian spirit.

After receiving Hochmann's letter, and after much Bible study, discussion, and prayer, eight persons chose to be baptized in the Eder River, which flows through Schwarzenau. In the first week of Aug., 1708, these eight were baptized by trine immersion to establish what Alexander Mack, Jr., later called a "covenant of good conscience with God." An officiant chosen by lot baptized Mack, who then baptized the others. The once loosely organized group became a *Gemeinde*, or congregational community. They were called the New Baptists of Schwarzenau.

As their first minister and elder, Mack led the small group in study of the Bible as they searched for guidance concerning basic patterns of church life, worship, and ritual. This was a period of experimentation. Some of their early practices were later abandoned: sexual continence in marriage, common ownership of possessions, and refraining from regular work. In 1713, Mack admitted that the New Baptists experienced much "contention," until they abandoned these "errors" in judgment. Patterns of religious belief were developed, patterns which continue to the present day; no coercion in religious matters, no creed but the New Testament, an emphasis on practical Christianity, baptism by trine immersion, the love feast service, the anointing of the sick, the holy kiss, and the congregational council meetings as a basis of church government or policy.

One of the most striking features of the New Baptists was their use of the ban. Based on Mt. 18:15-17, this mode of church discipline was strongly defended by Mack. Any member who sinned openly against another was visited by the elders of the church, who admonished the offending member to repent of the sin and turn from it. If repentance and reconciliation did not follow, this individual was asked to appear before the congregation to be placed under the ban. All other church members were then required to break off social relations with the person in the hope that repentance, forgiveness, and reconciliation might result.

One of Mack's beliefs was the doctrine of universalism, or universal restoration. Although he believed that all those who died unredeemed through Christ would be punished in the torment of hell, he did not maintain the "the torture should continue entirely without end." He could not find the idea of eternal damnation "sustained by the Scriptures." Mack felt strongly that the power of divine love would eventually be triumphant and that all persons would some day be united with God. However, in Mack's understanding, those restored to God after death would never attain the high state of bliss possible to those who chose to follow Christ in life.

From 1708-15, the Schwarzenau congregation grew rapidly. Mack helped it develop a pattern of organization which provided within its structure opportunity for continued spiritual growth, self-correction, and constant renewal. Not gifted with Hockmann's oratorical flair, Mack led the early Brethren with patience, perseverance, and organizational skill. During this period Hochmann, who had returned from prison to live in Schwarzenau until his death in 1721, became very critical of the Schwarzenau Baptists for starting a new sect. Attacks by other Pietists, the established church, and government officials of other principalities were also common. Yet Count Henrich Albrecht of Sayn-Wittgenstein-Hohenstein continued his protection of these people because of his own pietistic sympathies and his high regard for Alexander Mack.

In 1711, Mack was invited on two occasions to conduct baptismal services in the Marienborn area, near Dudelsheim, where Peter Becker lived. He returned a third time for the same purpose in 1713 but was permanently expelled from the area for breaking the law. In 1713, Eberhard Ludwig Gruber, a leader in the Community of True Inspiration, a rival pietistic group in the Marienborn area, debated with Mack on baptism, the ban, and the exclusivism of the Schwarzenau Baptists. This debate was printed as *Grundforschende Fragen (Basic Questions)*, the first publication by the New Baptists. This was followed by Alexander Mack's *Rechte und Ordnungben (Rights and*

Ordinances) in 1715.

During the years that Mack and his family lived at Schwarzenau, the congregation grew from eight to more than two hundred. Three children were born to the Macks: a daughter who died in infancy, Christina, and Alexander, Jr. During the years from 1715 to 1720, however, life for the Schwarzenau Baptists became increasingly difficult. Growth had virtually ceased because of competition from a large congregation of Inspirationists. Opportunities for employment were sparse. Many had scarcely enough to eat. Mack's own inheritance had been exhausted, and surrounding rulers were pressuring Count Henrich to change his policy of tolerance for religious dissenters. In view of these factors Mack and his community considered emigration. They were encouraged by Peter Becker, who had migrated with a group of Brethren from Krefeld to Pennsylvania in 1719.

In 1720, forty Brethren families migrated from Schwarzenau to the province of Friesland in the Netherlands, where they were warmly received by the Mennonite congregation in the village of Surhuisterveen. They found work in the peat fields and on surrounding farms. For shelter they built small homes out of peat. Mack continued his leadership in the community, baptizing and solemnizing marriages as occasion required. One of the weddings he performed in Holland was that of his son Johannes to Anna Margarethe Sudere in 1725.

Unfortunately, the economic situation did not improve. Wages were low, and the peat bogs were being depleted. Some of the Brethren were so poor that they had to accept charity from the Dutch Collegiants. In 1727, some relief came when Mack received another inheritance from his father-in-law, Johann Valentin Kling. Since the economic situation in Friesland was not promising and there was little opportunity for evangelization, the Brethren decided to migrate to America. This was not a unanimous decision and about half chose to remain in Europe. In the spring of 1729 these new emigrants left Surhuisterveen for Rotterdam, where Mack arranged for their voyage on a ship called the *Allen*. It sailed in late June, arriving in Philadelphia on Sept. 15, 1729.

Soon after his arrival in Germantown, where Peter Becker's group of immigrants had established a congregation in 1723,

Mack was made presiding elder of the congregation, which flourished under his leadership. The most perplexing problem confronting Mack in the New World was the refusal of Conrad Beissel, a minister at Conestoga, to recognize the leadership of Mack or any of the other Brethren leaders. On several occasions Mack sought unsuccessfully to heal this breach, which led to the development of the Ephrata Community. Yet Mack also had some very rich experiences at Germantown. His oldest son, Johann Valentin, was married to Maria Hildebrand in 1730; he welcomed his friends Abraham Dubois (1732) and Johannes Naas (1733) to the New World; and he participated in organizing several congregations.

Mack died at the age of fifty-five on Feb. 19. Many among the German-speaking people of Pennsylvania mourned his passing. He was interred in the Upper Burying Ground at Germantown, with a small marker designating his grave. George N. Falkenstein, pastor of the Germantown congregation, found Mack's grave in the old cemetery in 1894 and, with the consent of the Mack family, moved the remains to the present location.

Not seeking personal honor, Mack wrote very little about himself. Not seeking power, he did not become a dominating leader. Not being a charismatic or flamboyant person, others did not write about him. Yet, today, he is honored for his rich spiritual legacy to the family of Brethren churches. In Schriesheim, a street is named for him. In Schwarzenau, a school and a street bear his name. In America, a college library and a camp are named for him. But the greatest honor of all is the devotion of many to the practical Christian commitment he exemplified.

A compassionate person, he freely gave his inheritance to his brothers and sisters in need. A humble person, he refused the honors of the world, asking that even his grave be unmarked. A man of peace, he did not participate in war or violence. Open to new understandings of the Scriptures, he rejected the limitation of creeds and binding theologies. A practical person, he believed the Christian life is best expressed in the voluntary discipline of a loving, Christian community. In 1860, James Quinter fittingly described Mack as a "primitive follower of Christ."

William G. Willoughby

Mack's Personal Bible

Alexander Mack's personal Bible, which is preserved in the library of Bridgewater College, has between twenty and thirty leaves of blank paper bound with it at its beginning and end. On many of these pages Mack wrote comments inspired by his study of the Scriptures. The Bible, in Luther's German translation, was of small size, and was printed in 1723 in Lemgo, Germany. John S. Flory, who secured it for the Bridgewater library, noted that the Bible, probably brought by Mack from Germany, was left with Alexander Mack, Jr., then, at his death, with the Germantown congregation, who later presented it to Philip Rothenberger, who, in turn, gave it to Henry Kurtz. Flory obtained the Bible from Kurtz's son.

Kenneth I. Morse

Pages 1 through 7 were reprinted from the Brethren Encyclopedia, Inc.

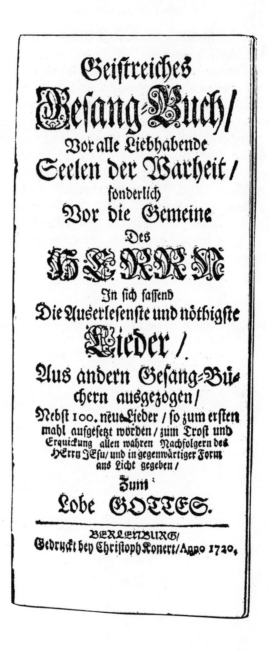

First Brethren hymn book published in 1720
in Berleburg, Germany (near Schwarzenau).

The First
Brethren Tract

During the summer of 1708, the first group of Brethren sponsored the writing of the following "open letter" or tract which was then circulated among the Pietists in the Palatinate region of southern Germany. Though it says that the writer was chosen by lot, it might be surmised that the actual writer was Alexander Mack, since he was the only one of the eight to publish any subsequent writings. This letter is extremely important in that it sets forth the Biblical and theological basis of the Brethren movement.

To All Those Beloved Called in Christ Jesus. Greetings!

Under the providence of God, in Christ Jesus the beloved, I announce and make known to the brethren beloved in God the wonderful divine ordinance which has revealed itself among brethren through their manifest confession about the true baptism. According to the Holy Scriptures, Jesus Christ, our Savior, received this true baptism from John the Baptist. When John, however, refused our dear Savior said, ". . . for thus it is fitting for us to fulfil all righteousness" [Matthew 3:15]. After he had been baptized, a voice from heaven called, "This is my beloved son, with whom I am well pleased [Matthew 3:17]. Listen to him" [Matthew 17:5]. John bore record saying, "I saw the Spirit descend as a dove from heaven, and it remained on him" [John 1:32].

I must first describe the beginning, when all of us, in varying numbers of years ago (indeed, one experienced a strong agitation of the heart already five years ago) expressed to several brethren: "You men, dear brethren. We must be baptized according to the teachings of Jesus Christ and the apostles." However, when this was opposed, it was passed over, but was not completely erased from our hearts. At various times I had an occasion to admit or realize before God and my conscience that it would still occur, and I was assured of it in my heart. In the past two years the other brethren were moved in their consciences that they must be baptized, but none of us knew of the others' concern. Quite by accident, when two foreign brethren visited us, that which was in our hearts was revealed. Our inner joy increased and we were strengthened in the Lord not to be negligent, and to come together in the fear of the Lord. Each one revealed and opened the depths of his heart. As we found that we all agreed with one spirit in this high calling, we have decided to announce this to our beloved brethren through an open letter. This is to see whether they also find themselves convinced in their hearts to help confirm this high calling to the pride and glory of our savior Jesus Christ, and to follow the Creator and Fulfiller of our faith. We drew lots, and the lot has fallen on the most unworthy.

Dear brethren, please have patience with this simple letter, as the dear Savior and Redeemer has patience with all of us, and hears and sustains us in His long-suffering.

I also want to remind the dear brethren that we must publicly profess that which Christ Jesus taught and did without hesitation or fear of men. We need not be ashamed and must above all suffer and endure all things with rejoicing.

"Joy! Joy! More joy! Christ prevents all suffering. Bliss! Bliss! More Bliss! Christ is the sum of grace!"

Concerning baptism, Christ, the first-born, is our forerunner, of whom the apostles and many thousands, testified with their blood that Jesus Christ was the Son of the living God. Now Jesus did not only teach, but also acted and commanded, saying to His disciples: "Go therefore and make disciples of all nations (and make known to them Jesus, the Son of God, that they may believe on Him, that He is the same), baptizing them in the name of the Father and of the Son and of the Holy Spirit, teaching them to observe all that I have commanded you" (Matthew 28 [19, 20]). Dear brethren! What is then better than being obedient and not despising the commandments of the Lord Jesus Christ, the King of all Glory? This, especially as we have left all sects because of the misuses concerning infant baptism, communion, and church system, and unanimously profess that these are rather man's statutes and commandments, and therefore do not baptize our children, and testify that we were not really baptized.

We should, however, remind ourselves of our baptismal covenant, and profess at the same time that it is man's commandment and teaching established after the statutes of the world, and does not follow simply the teaching of Jesus Christ. Oh, beloved brethren in the Lord, we will not be able to meet the test at that time when the Lord [*Hausherr*] will come and require from us the obedience which He has commanded of us. We have been unfaithful servants, as we knew, recognized, and professed the will of the dear Lord. Oh, there is still time today, dear brethren, before the sun of justice sets and the time breaks upon us of which Jesus says that one can work no more! Is it not highly necessary that we go to meet the Son of God on the holy path, and kiss Him, before His wrath is kindled?

Dear brethren, we cannot err, as He—the Way, the Truth and the Eternal Life—goes before us, and His teaching, namely Jesus Christ's, is sealed by His blood. His disciples have loyally followed Him and sealed it with their blood. Saint John faithfully explains to us in his second epistle that many deceivers have come into the world, and gives us the sign that whosoever does not remain in the teaching of Christ has no God. However, whosoever does remain in the teaching of Jesus Christ has both the Father and the Son. When we consider the eternal providence of God, which stands so clearly in the written teaching of Jesus Christ despite all controversy, does not this also seem a great miracle, that the almighty God so cares for us that we have a sure guide, and that a light always appears for us in the darkness? May God be eternally praised and glorified for His goodness, grace, and mercy, which He still evidences even to this hour.

In the second chapter of the Acts of the Apostles, it says that the multitude was so convinced by the sermon of Peter that they spoke, " 'Brethren, what shall we do?' And Peter said to them, 'Repent, and be baptized every one of you in the name of Jesus Christ . . .,' " and it is added, "For the promise is to you and to your children and to all that are far off, every one whom the Lord our God calls to Him" [Acts 2:37-39]. Now the apostles remained single-mindedly obedient and did not lay any emphasis on whether the Holy Spirit came to the persons before or after the baptism; rather, they remained firmly by the commandment of their Father and baptized those who had shown themselves repentant. This needs little proof, dear brethren, as the entire New Testament is full of it. It can, however, easily be seen that this is no slight or poor matter which can be taken lightly. It cannot possibly be that all obviously disorderly persons are accepted for baptism, when it is known that they are without true remorse and repentance.

There is also an exact relationship and brotherly discipline, according to the teaching of Jesus Christ and His apostles. When a person does not better himself, after faithful warning, he must be expelled and cannot be treated any more as a brother. We are truly assured that our Lord Jesus Christ, who at that time was given power and might in heaven and on the earth, is the initiator of our action, and will know how to carry it through wisely, and also provide here the one and the other to whom He will entrust wisdom and understanding. The ways of the Lord will then be orderly prepared, without giving offense and annoyance to the God-loving brethren and sisters. For the world, however, Christ and His disciples are a stumbling block and an annoyance, and it takes offense at the Word on which they are founded.

Dear brethren, it will certainly not require much more proof, as each one who is from God will be taught everything by the anointing, and will well understand the importance of baptism. Paul writes, Romans 6, "Do you not know that all of us who have been baptized into Christ Jesus were baptized into his death? We were buried therefore with him by baptism into death, so that as Christ was raised from the dead by the glory of the Father, we too might walk in newness of life" [3 and 4]. This is then the covenant of a good conscience with God, as Peter writes in First Peter 3:21 and explains very clearly that as the great flood cleansed the first world, so they have explained baptism, that from now on, all of the old sins and uncleanliness shall be washed away through baptism. For as a person is cleansed outwardly through water, so is the inner person cleansed through the blood of Jesus Christ in faith. The Holy Spirit gives His testimony thereto. These are the three witnesses on earth, of which St. John speaks (I John [5]:8).

I am quite convinced that you, dear brethren, are more familiar with the Holy Scriptures about this than I am, concerning Jesus Christ's teaching, action, life, and conduct. Your hearts will be, with ours, so mightily convinced that if an angel came from heaven and proclaimed something different we would not accept it. I do not doubt that some one could ignore this ordinance, and consider it unnecessary without the loss of his salvation if grounded in God. I also do not doubt that some out of folly for their own opinions may fail to do as our Lord Jesus Christ has done. But as Christ our head and keeper lowered himself into the water, so must we of necessity, as His members, be immersed with Him. Moreover, we do not write one point which is not from the teachings of Christ and His apostles out of the freedom of conscience which each one has. It may be that God has revealed to us, where possibly presumption is practiced. We live in the appearance of good and simple work and wish to eat our own bread in quiet conduct according to the teaching of St. Paul, the apostle. Where, however, God places different work on a brother, which may well be harder than physical work, then each one should attend to his own work to which God has called him, in the fear of the Lord. That I would like to have someone to be as I am, is very deceptive, for each should live according to his calling.

So then, if some more brethren wish to begin this high act of baptism with us out of brotherly unity according to the teachings of Christ and the apostles, we announce in humbleness that we are interceding together in prayer and fasting with God. We will choose him whom the Lord gives as the baptizer as God will reveal to us. If we then begin in the footsteps of the Lord Jesus to live according to His commandment, then we can also hold communion together according to the commandment of Christ and His apostles in the fear of the Lord. We now wish from the bottom of our hearts, grace, peace, and love for all brethren, from God our Father in Jesus Christ, His beloved Son, through the Holy Spirit. May the triune God seal, strengthen, found, and confirm His eternal truth in our hearts, that we may highly respect all that which is commanded through God. Let nothing depart from our hearts, but rather let us think upon it, talk about it, and also tell our children, that they also learn to observe the commandments and witness of God. Yes, the

Lord God of our fathers, the God of Abraham, be praised, the God of Isaac, and of Jacob, be highly exalted, and His name be glorified to the end of the world. Amen.

[Summer, 1708]   [One of the first eight]

Letter to
Count Charles August

On August 21, 1711, Alexander Mack baptised the daughter of Eva Elizabeth Hoffman in the river at Dudelsheim, contrary to the orders of the ruler, Count Charles August. On September 4, the widow Hoffman and Mack were expelled from the territory. On September 5, Alexander Mack wrote a two page letter to the Count justifying his baptism of the girl and protesting the harsh judgment on the widow and her daughter. Mack also expands the letter to include important statements that further explain and illuminate early Brethren theology. The letter is still preserved in the archives at the castle at Budingen and is frequently shown to Brethren visitors. This is the only letter known written in Mack's hand and with his signature.

Gracious Lord and Count:

An order has been published by the chancery of the lord count, first, that Eva Liz [Eva Elizabeth Hoffmann], a poor widow, must leave the territory together with her daughter, and that I too must leave the territory of the gracious lord, anyone sheltering me overnight to be fined five *florins*. I find myself impelled, therefore, to write these few lines to the lord count, to ask him to reconsider seriously before God, the judge of the living and the dead, whether this proceeding is according to the will of God, who established the authorities to punish the wicked and protect the good.

In the first place, Eva Liz was indeed at the chancery and was examined; however, she was not found guilty of any misdeed for which the authorities and justice had the right to persecute her. In the second place, I was not even examined, let alone asked what my faith was, much less found guilty of any misdeed. Such a procedure, firstly, is counter to the Jewish law, John 7:51, where Nicodemus says: "Does our law judge a man without first giving him a

15

Gnädiger Herr und Graff

Weilen von Herrn Graffen seiner Cantzley ein befehl ergangen, erstlich dass
die Eva Liss, eine arme Wittib, sambt ihren Töchtern, auss dem Lande weichen soll.
Und ich solle auch auss des gnädigen Herrn seinem Lande, wo mich aber in seinem
Lande über nachtes solle 5 fl straff erlegen, so finde ich mich gezwungen, dieses we-
nige, dem Herrn Graffen zu überschreiben, und ihme wohl zu bedencken geben, vor Gott
dem Richter der Lebendigen und der Todten, ob dieses verfahren, gehet nach dem willen Gottes
welcher die Obrigkeit gesetzet dass böse zu straffen und dass gutte zu beschützen.
Vors erste ist zwar die Eva Liss auff der Cantzley gewesen, und verhört worden
aber doch keine übel Taht können überwiesen werden, worüber eine Obrigkeit
recht macht hätte, sie zu verfolgen, vors ander bin ich nicht ein mahl verhöret
worden, oder nur gefragt wass mein glaube sey, viel weniger überwiesen, einer
übel Taht, solches verfahren streitet erstlich wieder dass Jüdische gesetz, Johan 7 Cap
V. 51, da sagte Nicodemus, richtet unser gesetz auch einen menschen, ehe man ihn verhöret
und erkennet wass er thut, ja es streitet auch wieder die heydnische recht, actor 25
Cap. V. 16, da sagte Festus. es wäre nicht der Römer weise einen Menschen umzubring-
en ehe der verklagte habe seine Kläger gegenwärtig. Und raum empfangen sich der an-
Klage zu verantworten, ja vom Christenthum will ich nichtes melden, dass ein Christ durch
den geist Christi solches thun könte, wass aber nun mein verbrechen ist will ichs bekennen
frey und offentlich. dass Jesus Christus der König aller Könige, und Herr aller Herren.
dass einige wass wir thun also haben will, dass der Sünder solle busse thun, und an
den Herrn Jesum glauben, und solle auff seinen glauben, sich tauffen lassen im wasser.
und solle dan alles suchen zu halten, wass er Jesus befohlen, und in seinem Testament
offentlich hinderlassen, thun wir nun hierinnen unrecht, wieder dass grosse gebote worde
heyliger Schrifft, es sey in lehr leben und wandel, so wollen wir uns ja gerne weisen
lassen, kan uns aber niemand dieses erweisen, mit gründ der heyligen schrifft, und
man uns doch verfolget, so wollen wir zwar gerne alles leyden, und dulten, um der
lehr Jesu Christi willen, so wollen wir appelliren allein, an den oberrichter Jesu Christi; welcher
am Tage der offenbahrung recht richten wird. Und einem jetlichen nach seinen wercken
vergelten, ohne ansehung der persohn, wan nun Jesus sagen wird, Matt 25 Cap zu
denen zur linken, gehet hin ihr verfluchter, weilen sie deine glieder [illegible] nicht gespeiset
und wie es ferner lautet, oh wass wird er sagen, zu denen die sie ohne recht und ohne
verhörung verfolget haben, die werden sagen müssen o ihr berge fallet über uns, und
ihr hügel bedecket uns, dan wir können nicht bestehen, vor dem der auff dem stuhl sitzet
darum ergehet mein unterthänigstes ersuchen, an gnädigen Herrn, er wolle doch alles
wass jetzund in seinem Lande geschicht, nach heyliger schrifft wohl prüffen und unter-
suchen, weilen er auch eine unsterbliche seele hatt. Und der mahl eins, vor Jesu dem

geschrieben ... 5. herbstmonat 17 11.

D. Alexander Mack, im
glid in ... Christi

hearing and learning what he does?" Yes, it is also counter
to the Gentile justice, Acts 25:16, where Festus says ". . .
it was not the custom of the Romans to give up any one
before the accused met the accusers face to face, and had
opportunity to make his defense concerning the charge laid
against him." Yes, I will not mention anything about
Christendom, that a Christian could, through the spirit of
Christ, do such a thing.

Now I will freely and publicly confess that my crime is that
Jesus Christ, the King of kings and Lord of lords, desired
that we do what we are doing—that the sinner shall repent
and believe in the Lord Jesus and should be baptized in
water upon his confession of faith. He should then seek to
carry out everything Jesus has commanded and publicly
bequeathed in His Testament. If we are doing wrong herein
against the revealed word of the Holy Scriptures, be it in
teaching, way of life, or conduct, we would gladly receive
instruction. If, however, no one can prove this on the basis
of the Holy Scriptures, and yet persecutes us despite this,
we would gladly suffer and bear it for the sake of the
teachings of Jesus Christ.

Therefore we would only appeal to the Supreme Judge,
Jesus Christ, who will judge rightly on the day of revelation,
and repay everyone according to his works, without regard
to persons. Then Jesus will say, Matthew 25 [verse 41], to
those on the left, "Depart from me, you cursed," because
they had not fed His flock, and as the text continues. Oh,
what will He say to those who have persecuted unjustly and
without giving a hearing! They will have to say, "Oh,
mountains, fall on us, and, hills, cover us, because we cannot
stand before Him who sits on the throne." Therefore I am
making my humble appeal to the gracious lord that he might
test according to the Holy Scriptures and investigate
thoroughly everything that now goes on in his territory. For
he, too, has an immortal soul, and will have to give account
one day before Jesus, the supreme liege lord, by whom he
was placed in authority in his territory, about the way he
governed his territory—whether it was according to sacred
order or not.

The whole earth is the Lord Jesus'. He has final power over
all the elements. He who molests His members molests
Jesus Himself. How can it be justified when members of the

Lord Jesus are prevented in their wish to baptize themselves in water after confession of faith, and to testify that Jesus is the true prophet to whose teachings they willingly submit; this, when they reject and abjure the devil, the world, and all evil, and lead exemplary lives before God and man. How can the poor Baptists help it that it is such an unusual performance, and that because of the harmful and [later-]introduced infant baptism, the true baptism of repentant sinners after their confession of faith commanded by Jesus has become so strange and obscure that even the chosen ones are almost offended and repelled by it?

It is probably not unknown to the lord count that for some time infant baptism was testfied against publicly and in books, and that it is still being testified against in his territory from the public pulpit. Should there then be no baptism, because infant baptism is invalid? Far be it, for Jesus commanded it very earnestly, Matthew, chapter 28, and Mark, chapter 16 [verse 16], and said: "He who believes and is baptized will be saved . . . ." What Jesus has ordained cannot be intentionally changed or broken by any person without loss of eternal salvation. If, however, true baptism brought no cross with it, but rather a good life, honor, and comfort as does infant baptism, the learned theologians would undoubtedly know how to support it from the Holy Scriptures. As, however, true baptism brings with it all sorts of contempt, and one cannot be a friend of the world at the same time, they say, against their own consciences, that it is an outward work not essential for salvation. Meanwhile, they allow the poor Christians to proceed under great difficulty, while they follow along living very comfortably with a doctrine which indeed keeps them from and avoids the cross.

I do not wish to annoy through writing too much, but rather close herewith, and leave it to the judgment of the lord count. As far as I am concerned, however, I do not complain at all about having to leave the territory, because I had planned to leave anyway. But because of Eva Liz, who is a poor widow, I humbly ask again that a little more consideration be given her. Should I, nevertheless, enter the territory again, I offer to defend my faith, if it is desired. If I can be shown by the learned theologians to be in error in some points, I will be happy to be instructed. If it is not possible, I ask again for understanding, for there has otherwise been much disorder in this county already.

I wish, meanwhile, for the lord count blessings from God and grace and divine light for his government, that he, too, may attain a good standing under the Kingdom of Christ. I heartily wish this for him, and remain his humble,

Written the fifth of the   Alexander Mack,
Fallmonth [September], 1711.   a member of Jesus Christ.

Basic

Questions

The First major statement of Brethren beliefs by Alexander Mack was published in 1713, likely by a printer in Berleburg, located about 10 miles from Schwarzenau. The form of the publication presents a series of 40 questions supposedly submitted by Eberhard Louis Gruber who later became one of the main leaders of the Inspirationists. The Inspirationists were neighbors of the Brethren at Schwarzenau for awhile, later moving to several locations in Germany and Pennsylvania, finally settling in Amana, Iowa. The answers to the 40 questions constitutes the Brethren response to a number of concerns raised by outsiders, whether by Gruber or not. The book was printed in America by Christopher Saur in 1774. It has since been reprinted several times, both in the original German and in several English translations.

Eberhard Louis Gruber's

Basic Questions

which were especially submitted to be answered by the

New Baptists of the Wittgenstein Area

along with the accompanying

Brief and Simple Answers to the Same,

previously published in manuscript by an

ARTLESS MEMBER

of the church at Wittgenstein

and now publicly printed at the request of many.

[GRUBER]

In God Beloved Friends and Fellow Pilgrims:

There have been several persons who have desired a somewhat more definite explanation and report about your new baptism and church fellowship, especially since that which has been said or even written about it from time to time has still left them in great uncertainty. In order to learn about your opinion more thoroughly and accurately and thereby dispel any further doubt in regard to it, these candid and herewith-presented questions are submitted to you. We expect your clear and frank answers upon these soon.

[MACK]

Dear Friends:

You have requested from us in love our motives. The Apostle Peter teaches believers (1 Peter 3:15) that they must always be ready to give an answer to anyone who calls them to account for the hope that is in them. For these reasons, we have not been able to evade this, but rather have very briefly answered these submitted questions in a simple fashion with frankness in love and in the certainty of faith. We wish to leave them to your examination before God.

QUESTION 1: Do you maintain that for over one thousand years there has been no true and genuine baptism, and, consequenty, no true church on earth?

ANSWER: We maintain and believe that at all times God has had His church which observed the true baptism and ordinances. This was, however, always hidden from the unbelievers and often consisted of but few members. Despite this, the gates of hell could never prevail against the church of the Lord Jesus. It can also be proved from the histories that God has caused His ordinancees to be revealed as a witness to the unbelievers at all times.

QUESTION 2: Could the church of God have existed at any time and in any manner even with but few members, without the original and outward ordinance of baptism, as the Israelite church (according to Joshua 5:5-7) existed for considerable time in the wilderness without practicing circumcision?

ANSWER: The church of Christ is ordained in no other way by the true Master-Builder, Jesus Christ, than that it should observe His baptism and ordinances. Christ indeed ordained everything perfectly in His congregation or church through His apostles and teachers, and sufficiently confirmed it by signs and miracles. For this reason, the fact is incontestable that a congregation or church of Christ could never have existed without the baptism and ordinances as commanded by the true Founder.

We do not deny that there could have been souls who were attracted in secret to the church of Christ. Whether, however, they followed and publicly professed Christ, or whether they preferred the honor of the world to the honor of God, we will not determine. As far as the Israelite church is concerned, it can be clearly seen that while in the wilderness the children had to bear the reproach of Egypt and suffer for the transgressions of their fathers! However, as soon as they were about to enter the promised land, and before they took the first city, Jericho, they first all had to be circumcised. God said to Joshua (5[:9]: "This day I have rolled away the reproach of Egypt from you." Only after this did they dare to celebrate the Passover and not before.

This is then a sign for us that as long as we walk in the wilderness and in great disorder and uncertainty—even though we have gone out of Egypt and have been rescued from gross sins by the mighty hand of God—we can still neither enter the house of God nor break the bread in the communion of Jesus and His members. God demands also of us that we should be baptized; He will indeed demand it of everyone, although perhaps in secret, if men will only listen to the inner voice and obey it with denial of self.

QUESTION 3: Did, then, the church of God here on earth completely cease to exist during the time that the early ordinance of baptism was no longer observed?

ANSWER: If the early ordinance of baptism had ceased to exist, then, of course, the church of Christ would also have ceased to exist. Even if there had been souls here and there who lamented the great apostasy, they could not have been called a church. However, we believe, and it can also be shown from the ancient histories, that the early form of baptism as ordained by the ordinance of Christ has never ceased to exist. Consequently, the church has likewise never ceased to exist, even if there were but few members.

QUESTION 4: How would you reconcile this with the

promise of Jesus (Matthew 16:18) that the gates of hell shall not prevail against the church, and (28:20) that He will be with them always to the close of the age, and similar declarations?

ANSWER: This has already been answered because we believe that the gates of hell have *not* prevailed against the church of Christ; it has endured and will endure until the close of the age.

QUESTION 5: What, then, do you think about the salvation of those undeniable witnesses of truth who appeared from century to century, even during that time? Were they not members of Christ and His fellowship or true church which is united by the living spirit, just because they had not been baptized in accordance with the original ordinance?

ANSWER: Christ says (Matthew 7[:16]): "You will know them by their fruits." We believe that writing fine books and even prophesying are not the fruits of a good Christian, by which alone he is recognized. We cannot, therefore, consider a person to be a Christian for that alone. Yet, we will not judge anyone. Since we did not know those men in their lifetime, we leave them to their God. Neither all their writing nor even their prophesying can make us suspicious of the teaching of Jesus. We cannot consider them to be the church of Christ just because of their prophesying, if they did not walk in the teaching of Jesus, in baptism and the other ordinances.

QUESTION 6: Are you not of the opinion that the baptismal ceremony which has so long been neglected must be re-established in these later times, and if so, why do you think so? Has not rather the all-wise God permitted this ceremony (which is not exactly part of the essence of Christianity) to be done away with, like the circumcision of the Old Covenant, for the very reason that it is as yet imperfect and does not yet make anything perfect, so that He could introduce a new economy and housekeeping of the pure spirit for His people, as all prophetic promises have foretold?

ANSWER: We are of the opinion and believe as the apostle writes (Hebrews 7:12): "For when there is a change in the priesthood, there is necessarily a change in the law as well." As long as the Levitical priesthood existed, just that long no one dared to annul the law, or circumcision, without incurring God's grave punishment and displeasure. However, when Christ came He introduced a law of life as the eternal High Priest and Son of God. He annulled the first law because it was too weak and could not make anyone perfect. He secured eternal redemption, revealed the paths to the Holy of Holies, and gave only laws of life. He confirmed His will or testament with His blood, so that we believe and profess that if an angel came from heaven and attempted to reveal another or better gospel, the angel would be accursed, according to the witness of Paul (Galatians 1:18).

Therefore, we believe that the teaching of Jesus the crucified must be kept until He himself shall come again and take vengeance with flaming fire upon those who were not obedient to His gospel, according to Paul's witness (2 Thessalonians 1:8). For this reason, then, the teachings of Jesus are rightly to be observed by believers in these days. However, there are no commandments for unbelievers.

QUESTION 7: Are you not compelled to recognize and admit that in that particular case [baptism] a direct divine calling is necessary and required for the re-establishment, just as well as for its first institution, which calling, according to the testimony of the Scriptures and the general confessions, has always been present at such great reformations of the church?

ANSWER: We do indeed believe that a direct calling and impelling by the Spirit of God is necessary for the practicing of the teachings of Christ. That, however, this calling must be confirmed and manifested before men by signs or miracles, we will not presume to dictate to God. If the calling is of God, it is sufficient, whether men believe it or not. This must be left up to the individual.

QUESTION 8: Can any one of you stand up who is willing to state, upon his conscience and responsibility in the hour of his death and on the Day of Judgment, that he had received such a direct calling from God to re-establish the ordinance of baptism which was so long neglected, and with it to form an entirely new church of Christ here on earth such as has not existed since the time of the apostles and the early Christians?

ANSWER: When the Pharisees sent from Jerusalem and

asked John whether he was the Christ or a prophet because he was baptizing, he answered: "I baptize you with water (for repentance), but among you stands one whom you do not know; he will baptize you with the Holy Spirit and with fire" [John 1:26; Matthew 3:11]. We likewise say in simplicity that we baptize in water only upon faith in Christ, who lets His voice be heard in the hearts of men in these days. Oh, if we would only follow Him and would know Him rightly, He would be the only one, and remain so forever, who shall establish, sanctify, and cleanse a church in this time with the "washing of water with the word" (Ephesians 5:26). No man would dare to appropriate this for himself, or declare before men that he was sent by God to establish a church, but he would gladly leave the honor to God. Even though God may use some as special instruments for this, they only need to be tested whether they are sent by God, as John says (3:34): "For he whom God has sent utters the words of God."

QUESTION 9: Of what does this direct calling consist? How can you justify and present this to the hearts and consciences of those who are still among the sects, as well as to those who have already withdrawn from them, for their outward or inward conviction?

ANSWER: The direct calling consists in the fact that the person is made inwardly exceedingly certain of it by the Spirit of God, and is not concerned whether men believe it or not. Jesus himself says (John 6:43, 44): "Do not murmur among yourselves. No one can come to me unless the Father who sent me draws him." It is equally true that no one can come to the teaching of Christ unless he lets himself be drawn by the Father. Whoever follows the guiding of the Father will easily recognize who the called and elect faithful are.

QUESTION 10: May it not properly be expected after the truth that if this work were indeed from God and you had received this direct divine calling to it, well-meaning souls would have gathered by the thousands? Would not the same thing have happened as that which took place at the first Pentecost of the New Testament under the direction of the Spirit at that time, and through the power of Jesus Christ in and on the apostles of the Lord?

ANSWER: Christ says (Matthew 24) to His followers that

they should take heed especially in these days that no man lead them astray. He does not say that men will flock to His gospel by the thousands in such miserable times as these are, unfortunately, when love has grown cold in many hearts. Indeed, even the well-meaning souls do not come very willingly to the discipleship of Jesus, where all must be denied if Christ is to be followed rightly. On the contrary, Christ speaks of this time that the great abomination of desolation will be revealed. It only says that we must take refuge in the hills—that is, in the teachings of Jesus the crucified, which is exalted by all believers and is the city of God and the mountain of Zion, as stated in Hebrews 12:22, 23. Here, all true believers have always taken refuge. Many cannot even take their wives or children along, just as it happened to Lot, even though he was led by angels through a divine calling to escape destrucion. Despite this, his friends found it ridiculous; yes, he even had to leave his wife on the way. For this reason, Christ urges His followers very briefly to bear this in mind, saying (Luke 17:32): "Remember Lot's wife."

QUESTION 11: Is water baptism so absolutely necessary that positively no one can be saved without it, no matter how holy and irreproachable his belief and life are otherwise?

ANSWER: We believe and profess that in the Old and New Testaments blessing and salvation are promised only to the faithful. We can see the way in which the faithful have been minded and disposed at all times in the believing Abraham, the father of all the faithful. He was obedient to God in everything, and therefore obtained the promise because of his living faith which effected works of obedience. Hence, we believe that if a man lives in a holy and perfect way, and his life is effected by true faith in Christ, it will indeed be easier for him to have faith to be obedient to water baptism than it was for Abraham to sacrifice his son.

When, however, this person still argues with his God, saying "Of what use is this water for me?" this "holy life" is nothing but self-righteousness. Man seeks to establish it as did the Jews, about whom Paul speaks (Romans 10:9, 10). No salvation is promised to such selfish holiness. Christ is the fulfillment of the Law. Whoever believes in Him is justified. Faith in Christ produces obedience and submission to all of His words and commandments.

QUESTION 12: Does not the principal passage of Mark 16:16 prove the very contrary, where Jesus prudently says: ". . . he who does not believe (not he who is not baptized) will be condemned"?

ANSWER: We do indeed believe and profess that eternal life is not promised because of baptism, but only through faith in Christ (John 3:15, 18). Why should a believer not wish to do the will of Him in whom he believes? If it is the will of Christ that a believer should be baptized, then it is also the will of the believer. If he thus wills and believes as Christ wills, he is saved, even if it were impossible for him to receive baptism. Abraham was willing to sacrifice his son Isaac, but it did not happen; the son was not sacrificed. Yet obedience was fulfilled, and the blessing was received. Therefore, a believer who desires to be baptized, but cannot obtain it because of necessity—like the criminal on the cross—is still saved.

If, however, a man does not desire to be baptized, he is rightly to be judged as unbelieving and disobedient, not because of the baptism, but because of his unbelief and disobedience. Christ has rightly said, "He who believes . . ." [Mark 16:16]. If He had made salvation dependent on the water, men would be much more willing to be baptized, and retain their own will in other things. The Antichrist does this in assigning salvation to the water only, although the person lives otherwise as he pleases.

QUESTION 13: If water baptism is so absolutely necessary, why did Christ not mention it in His Sermon on the Mount when speaking of the Beatitudes (Matthew 5)? Why did He not make the least mention of it in His description of the judgment (Matthew 25), where He deals especially with all those who should be saved or condemned?

ANSWER: It is surprising how little men recognize the pure mind of God! Christ indeed speaks (Matthew 5) about many kinds of blessings. We might well ask from where such blessings may be obtained. Christ says: "Blessed are the meek . . ." [Matthew 5:5]. Now notice well how Christ calls (Matthew 11:28, 29), "Come to me . . . and learn from me." Therefore, we profess that Christ alone is the Savior. Whoever wishes to be blessed, as He preaches in Matthew 5, must necessarily accept Him in true faith, and must submit himself to Him in obedience, as clay in the hands of its potter. It is He who must make everything new and save all, and of Him all of the prophets have spoken. God himself refers to His Son.

Since then, Christ, as Savior and as the Good Physician, considers baptism necessary for believers, obedience to this commandment of baptism is also necessary for salvation. Even though Christ counts as blessed (Matthew 25) those who fed and clothed Him—and mentioned nothing of the new creature or rebirth about which He spoke (John 3), that without rebirth no one could enter the Kingdom of God, and at the latter place in turn did not say anything about visiting Him in prison or feeding His members—who would think that He counts as blessed in Matthew 25 those who were unreborn men or unbelievers, merely because of their outward works? Oh, no! Who would assume that they despised baptism? I believe that not a single person was among them who despised water baptism. There may have been some who were not baptized out of necessity, but not out of contempt for it.

QUESTION 14: How can you prove that John the Baptist was himself baptized, for he said to Christ (Matthew 3:14): "I need to be baptized by you, and do you come to me?" Or was he perhaps saved by a special exception?

ANSWER: Many questions could be asked in the same way: Where were Peter and John baptized, or where was this or that saint of the Old Covenant circumcised? More questions might be raised than would tend to edification toward God in faith. Paul records (1 Timothy 1[:4]) that there were even men who concerned themselves with endless genealogies. Nevertheless, we will also answer this in patience. John was indeed willing to be baptized by Christ, and desired this. We ascribe salvation to this faith, according to Scripture, and not to baptism. Even though it does not state explicitly in the Scriptures that he was baptized, at any rate it does say that he did not despise baptism. In addition, John will not be found among those who say, "Oh, of what use is water baptism for me?" Rather, he showed his obedience to Christ, as Abraham showed his obedience to God in the offering of his son. The son was not sacrificed, yet the obedience was fulfilled.

QUESTION 15: Were, then, all those who lived and died after the time of the early Christians who did not receive baptism in the original form completely lost and damned even though they faithfully observed the rules of Christ and true Christianity in all other respects—some even spending their blood and lives for it—only because they were content with their baptism received in infancy out of ignorance or lack of a higher motivation?

ANSWER: If they had had the same experience as Abraham when he offered his son, namely that they had the true faith in Jesus, which is the foundation of all the rules of true Christianity, they were certainly saved. They were certainly saved even if they had not obtained outward baptism, perhaps in times of persecution or because of other circumstances. However, if they thought that their infant baptism was valid, then they were of course ignorant of the fundamentals of the Christian religion. They will probably have lived up to the fundamentals of Christianity to a small degree or not at all. They will scarcely have achieved the new creation which alone is acceptable before God. Still, we will not judge those who lived many years ago, but leave them to their God. However, similar ignorance of men today who perhaps oppose baptism because of lack of knowledge will not help them at all on the Day of Revelation.

QUESTION 16: Does not the commandment of baptism apply also to children, as did the commandment of circumcision in the Old Covenant? Consequently are not children in danger of forfeiting their salvation as long as they are not baptized? Also, will they not be damned if they die without baptism?

ANSWER: Just as circumcision did not concern children before the eighth day—to have circumcised before that time would have even been a violation of circumcision—the baptism commanded of believers does not concern children before they are able to profess their faith. The eighth day of circumcision is a prefiguration of this.

QUESTION 17: Were children damned in the Old Covenant who died without having received circumcision? If so, how are the comforting words of David (2 Samuel 12:23) to be understood which he spoke about his child conceived with Bathsheba that died on the seventh day?

ANSWER: The children who died before the eighth day had violated the commandment of circumcision as little as the female infants who were not circumcised at all, which did not hinder their salvation in any way. Enoch led a godly life, attained many hundred years, and was not circumcised; yet he was obedient to God, for that was not demanded of him. This is the way of God's commandments: where there is no law, there is no violation; where there is no violation, there is no punishment.

QUESTION 18: At what age then are the children to be baptized? Is it not proper to use all diligence to help them to be baptized as early as at all possible, even in their infancy?

ANSWER: Children are to be presented to the Lord Jesus in prayer, but baptism should be delayed until they are able to prove and profess their faith. This may be considered the "eighth day" or the first day of the new creation of a person. If they were to be baptized in their state of ignorance, it would be as if the Jews had practiced circumcision before the eighth day. This would have been a violation of circumcision rather than an obedient act.

QUESTION 19: Are not the children as capable of being baptized as of having faith (according to Luke 1:41-44; Matthew 18:3; Luke 18:16, 17; 1 Corinthians 7:14, etc.) even though they do not know how to express this with many words as do the adults? Is this not in accordance with the Word (Mark 16:16) that it is not so much a matter of an easily deceptive oral profession of faith as the truth of faith itself?

ANSWER: There is only one example of this in Scripture. John was moved in his mother's womb through the Holy Spirit because he was a child of the promise and was to be a forerunner of the Lord. Yet, it is obvious that he could not have been circumcised in his mother's womb but only after he was born. Despite this, they waited with circumcision until the eighth day. Therefore, even the moving of Saint John did not cause a change in the plan of God concerning circumcision. Rather, he was circumcised like all other children on the eighth day.

It is exactly the same with baptism. Even if the children of believing parents were to move in their mothers' wombs, they would have to wait with baptism until they were born.

Again, once they were born, they would have to wait until they were moved by the Holy Spirit to desire baptism with specific words. Only then might they be baptized, because outward baptism requires an outward expression of desire, as may be seen from Christ himself (Matthew 3:13). This desire must be effected by the true faith in the Lord Jesus. Otherwise, it is not permissible to baptize a child. Salvation is not dependent upon the water, but only upon the faith, which must be proved by love and obedience.

QUESTION 20: Does it not run counter to the evangelical character of the New Covenant to make an outward ceremony indispensably necessary for salvation? Is this not rather identical with the doctrine of the old Law-zealots against whom Paul wrote so emphatically in his letters to the Galatians and the Colossians?

ANSWER: We do not make of outward baptism anything else than what is commanded by Scripture. Since it says that believers should be baptized, we consider it disobedience to oppose that which God has commanded. Whoever opposes God in one thing—even if it is as insignificant as outward baptism—such a person will be properly punished for this disobedience. However, I do not think that a single commandment of the Lord Jesus dare be considered insignificant, if we consider the power and might of the Sovereign without reluctance. Concerning that about which Paul wrote to the Galatians and Colossians, it has only to do with the laws of the servant Moses, because they were too weak (see Hebrews 7:18). The Galatians wanted to follow these laws in order to be spared the cross of Christ and to set aside the teaching of Jesus. Paul reminded them of the baptism when he wrote: "For as many of you as were baptized into Christ have put on Christ" (Galatians 3:27). Consequently, Paul is not at all against baptism, but rather for it.

QUESTION 21: If baptism is made an absolutely necessary commandment for salvation, will this not introduce a new papacy, and bring about salvation by works?

ANSWER: It has been testified sufficiently above that we do not seek to earn salvation with these simple works, but by faith in Christ alone. If it is to be a saving faith, it must produce works of obedience. Where that faith is not present which produces obedience (not according to the pope's doctrine and command but rather by the command of Jesus the crucified), then no salvation is promised for a single work done without faith.

QUESTION 22: Can the outward ban be an essential part of the church of Christ, when Christ himself did not practice or enforce it even upon Judas, who was wicked through and through?

ANSWER: The ban is an essential and necessary part of the church of Christ, as long as it remains in combat here in this wicked world among wolves and evil spirits. There can be no church of Christ without the ban. Otherwise, the devil and his leaven of wickedness would soon contaminate the good. The true believers have never rejected this, insofar as they have remained in the faith. They have considered it an evidence of divine grace and the great love and solicitude of God. They have used it as a firm wall around the church of the Lord.

Concerning Judas, we maintain that Christ did sufficiently exercise the ban upon him. He turned him over to Satan so that he hanged himself. The fact that he was not placed in the ban by Jesus before his outward act is not against the ban, but rather in its favor. This has always been the plan of God, as can be seen in Adam. He most probably had had contact with the Tempter before, but he was not driven from Paradise until he had actually eaten of the forbidden fruit. Similarly, Judas had earlier considered treachery, but the long-suffering Jesus had borne with him, tolerated him, and urged him to repentance, until evil finally gained the upper hand and committed the evil deed. After that, he came sufficiently under the ban of Christ. The ban was practiced properly upon Judas.

QUESTION 23: Is not the binding and loosing of the apostles a prerogative granted only to them, which dare not be usurped by anyone else?

ANSWER: That the loosing and binding is a special prerogative of the apostles is true. It is, however, of the following manner. Moses had a special prerogative in that the Law was revealed to the house of Israel through him, but despite this it was not a prerogative which meant that the Law was to die with the death of Moses; rather, the descendants submitted themselves in obedience, insofar as they were faithful to God, to that which was revealed by Moses in the house of God. Christ the true Householder, has likewise founded a church and household and has given to His apostles, as the elect witnesses, the prerogative that they should introduce the ordinances of the house of God and confirm them by signs and miracles. This was so that none of their descendants should presume to introduce other ordinances, perhaps out of impertinence or arrogance, but that they should willingly submit themselves to the ordinances by which the apostles were appointed the stewards over God's mysteries. Since, then, the ban was commanded by Christ and His apostles, their prerogative is rightly left to them. But the believers must subject themselves to it in faith, and exercise it without the respecting of persons.

QUESTION 24: Did Christ institute a universal law for the church of the New Testament with the words of Matthew 18:17, or did He not rather speak of it with special regard to the character of the Jews? Did He not, in addition, give His followers a completely different lesson in the following twenty-first and twenty-second verses?

ANSWER: We have shown above that Christ has given a universal law for His church with the words of Matthew 18:17. They are by no means annulled by the following twenty-first and twenty-second verses, but are rather confirmed by them, This is still more clearly expressed in Luke 17:4, where Christ says: ". . . if he (your brother) sins against you seven times in the day, and turns to you seven times, and says, 'I repent,' you must forgive him." Without the admission of the sin, there is no forgiveness of sin, not even by God. Just so must believers be minded that if the sinner admits his sin, he must be forgiven. If he does not acknowledge it, then the ban is rightly to be exercised, as Christ says (Matthew 28[:20]): ". . . teaching them to observe all that I have commanded you; and lo, I am with you always, to the close of the age."

QUESTION 25: Did the apostles ever forbid administering the necessary spiritual or physical services to a banned person?

ANSWER: The apostles have never forbidden the administering of the necessary spiritual or physical services to a banned sinner. Rather, the banned person should be called to repentance; if he does not listen or accept it, then one is at liberty. It is the same with physical things—if there is an abundance of goods and the banned person is in need, he should be shared with as necessary.

QUESTION 26: Have you, the New Baptists, ever had the same divine effect and result with some of those whom you have banned as did the apostles?

ANSWER: We firmly believe that the ban has an inner effect and result here and now with all those on whom we have exercised it according to the Word of God. On the Day of Revelation it will indeed become outwardly manifest if they have not repented during this time of grace. However, it has not yet happened that men were immediately struck dead as was Ananias. This was recorded only once even of the apostles. Many were put into the ban by the apostles, but no other died outwardly like this. Nevertheless, the power of the ban had its full effect upon them.

QUESTION 27: Is the true spiritual rebirth inseparable from water baptism?

ANSWER: The spiritual rebirth is nothing else than true and genuine obedience toward God and all of His command-ments. A reborn person will readily say with Christ (Matthew 3:15): ". . . it is fitting for us to fulfil all righteousness." We can, therefore, answer that the desire for obedience toward water baptism is inseparable from the true rebirth. If because of necessity, but not out of contempt or disobedience, water baptism does not take place, it will not be of harm for the rebirth.

QUESTION 28: Are all of those whom you baptize immediately reborn of God in truth?

ANSWER: That would indeed be a good baptism, if all those whom we baptize in water were truly reborn. It cannot be proved that all of those baptized by Christ and the apostles turned out well. If, however, true faith is present, and the Word is grasped or accepted in the water bath by faith, then a considerable rebirth or cleansing occurs in the "washing of water with the word" (Ephesians 5:26).

QUESTION 29: Could not a person be truly reborn even

before he is baptized, since water baptism—as you yourselves will not deny—does not insure the true, spiritual rebirth?

ANSWER: Adam was created in Paradise in the image of God. When he was disobedient to his God, he lost his divine stature and had to accept the curse and death because of his disobedience. Therefore, a person may, of course, have attained a goodly proportion of rebirth before water baptism. But unless he becomes ever more obedient and humble, he may very easily lose again that which he had previously attained. The food of the new creation, then, for its sustenance and growth, is true obedience to the Lord Jesus. If they do not eat this food—which is indeed the food of the new creation (John 4:34)—but eat the food of the serpent—which is disobedience in manifold wisdom and cleverness against the Word—then the same thing will happen to them as happened to Adam in Paradise. Since, then, water baptism is commanded by Christ, each reborn person must humble himself in obedience and fulfill this righteousness.

QUESTION 30: Is not the true brotherhood of Christians founded much rather upon rebirth than upon water baptism?

ANSWER: The true brotherhood of Christians has always been founded upon true faith and obedience to Jesus Christ and His gospel. Therefore, true brethren in Christ have never been able to refuse outward water baptism, because they observed it in their first-born Brother, who also commanded it of them. He, Christ himself, considers only those His brethren who do the will of God (Matthew 12:50).

QUESTION 31: Are not those who have proved their rebirth by their lives before God and man to be considered rightfully as brethren, even though they have not been baptized? (See Matthew 12:49, 50.)

ANSWER: We indeed consider brethren all those who prove their rebirth by their lives before God and man. However, they will not oppose water baptism, but will let themselves be baptized upon their faith and inner motivation. Christ himself considered only those His brethren who were His disciples, and who had been baptized. (See Matthew 12:49, 50 correctly.)

QUESTION 32: Can you testify before the countenance of Jesus Christ, the omniscient Searcher of hearts and Judge of the living and the dead, that you yourselves have always been one heart and one soul?

ANSWER: God does not require of us that we should be at this time in the perfection of one heart and one soul. We cannot say that we are completely one in spirit, but we must be one in purpose. That is, we must help one another until we all attain to the same faith and to that unity of fullness in faith of which Ephesians speaks (4:11-13). No one can say that the church at Jerusalem was one heart and one soul in the state of perfection. In the beginning they were united in their discipleship of Christ with denial of everything worldly. That they were not one in understanding may be seen in Acts 15:5, etc.

Those who came from Jerusalem taught differently about circumcision than did the apostles. They had great trouble in working toward unity. It is therefore surprising that this perfect unity is demanded of us in these dreadful days, in which darkness and gloom cover all peoples. Indeed, those who boast of the inward baptism of the spirit are so disunited that they show only ignorance and discord even in the plain and clear commandments of water baptism, as well as in other fundamental points of faith.

QUESTION 33: Do you not regard your church as superior to those of all other Baptist-minded [*Taufgesinnte*] of these or previous times, and if so, in which way and why?

ANSWER: It is true that we consider our church fellowship superior to these now-deteriorated Baptists [Mennonites], with whom we are acquainted, and whom we know. The reason is that they have deteriorated in doctrine and life, and have strayed far from the doctrine and life of the old Baptists [Anabaptist]. Many of them notice this and realize it themselves. We cannot answer concerning the previous Baptists, because we did not know them in life. We are completely agreed with them as far as their doctine is concerned, which does not teach anything in contradiction to the gospel.

QUESTION 34: What are your reasons for considering your newly established church, the practices of baptism, ban, etc, equal to those of the apostles, inasmuch as you can prove neither your divine calling, talents, nor results in your lives?

ANSWER: We consider ourselves far inferior to and still unworthy in the matter of power of working miracles, as compared to the apostles. Concerning the doctrine and the intention, we must pray to God that He might make us resemble the intention of the apostles, yes, even His Son Jesus.

QUESTION 35: Can and dare your teachers and elders bring the testimonies of their consciences before God that the Holy Spirit established them as shepherds in their churches to look after their flock as churches of God? Do they possess and can they demonstrate the spiritual gifts required and necessary for this, as given in Second Corinthians 6, etc.?

ANSWER: Of course, they must be able to bring it before God; otherwise they would not be true shepherds. They should not be worried or grieved if men do not believe this, but rather rejoice, if their names are cast out as evil by the people (Luke 6:22).

QUESTION 36: Must they not admit before God in their souls that many among them were much more loving, meek, humble, and so forth before their baptism than afterwards?

ANSWER: Our answer to this is "No," unless it would be for those who were cut off as withered branches, or unless this meant the simulated love which is feigned for the sake of bread or honor, and which does not punish sins and errors. This kind of love says: "Leave me alone in my own will, opinion, and actions, and I will leave you alone in yours; we will love each other and be brethren." If this is meant, then we confess that it is true. Unfortunately, we stayed long enough in this pernicious hypocritical love, while we were still among the Pietists. Now we have learned, and must continue to learn, that kind of love which hates and punishes wickedness and evil.

QUESTION 37: Is it not true that you began your new baptism with much uncertaintly and wavering and have continued in this way up to now? Has this not also been shown in other things, as, for example, you once rejected the married state, and then soon permitted it again—once did away with work, then introduced it again?

ANSWER: We have begun the baptism of the Lord Jesus in accordance with His command in great assurance of faith. The dear God has sustained and confirmed us in this to this day by His grace amidst great oppostion. We indeed can say with great certainty that those who believe should be baptized. But it is true that we had to continue discussions on marriage, work, yes, and still other matters, after the baptism. Before our baptism, when we were still among the Pietists, we were not taught otherwise by those who were deemed great saints. Therefore, we had much contention until we abandoned the errors which we had absorbed.

QUESTION 38: On which point, then, can the undoubted divinity of your new church be recognized before all others in the whole world?

ANSWER: We indeed have neither a new church nor any new laws. We only want to remain in simplicity and true faith in the original church which Jesus founded through His blood. We wish to obey the commandment which was in the beginning. We do not demand that undoubted divinity be recognized in our church fellowship. Rather, we would wish that undoubted divinity might indeed be recognized in Christ himself, and then in the church at Jerusalem. If this and its divinity in teaching, words, and commandments were to be acknowledged, then it could be determined whether a church has this divine teaching in it or not. If this is realized, then we think that it would be sufficient to recognize a church before all other churches in the whole world, if she is subject, as a true wife to her husband Christ, to His commands, yes, if it still strives to be even more submissive. Whoever has not known Christ in the divinity of His commandments will hardly recognize His church even if the twelve apostles were serving as its bishops and teachers.

QUESTION 39: Are you yourselves assured, and have you already received the eternal assurance in the divine test of fire, that God himself recogizes you and would have you recognized? How do you propose to prove this and make it credible?

ANSWER: We must certainly have assurance before God, as Paul describes it (Romans 5[:1, 2]): "Therefore, since we are justified by faith, we have peace through our Lord Jesus

Christ. Through him we have obtained access to this grace in which we stand, and we rejoice in our hope of sharing the glory of God." This assurance, however, is no longer promised, as it was also promised to the apostles, by the Lord Jesus (John 15:7): as long as they abide in Him, and His word abides with them, they are His rightful disciples. Whatever they asked for would be granted them. Thus it remains: he that is faithful in the teachings of Jesus, even to the end, will be saved.

QUESTION 40: Do you expect a better outcome for your church than that of the former Anabaptists? From where should this come? What is the assurance of your souls before and from God, who is impartial and who utterly humiliates and destroys all that is high and exalted, even all sects that pride and seek only themselves?

ANSWER: If we remain in the teaching of the New Testament, we expect this outcome, namely, that the fulfilment of our faith will be eternal life. In return for insignificant shame and suffering, we will obtain immeasurably momentous glory. We cannot testify for our descendants—as their faith is, so shall be their outcome. Nevertheless, we can say this, that the outcome of the former Baptists has turned out far better than the seed of L[uther], C[alvin], and also that of the C[atholics]. These have had a completely wild, yes, bestial outcome, which is self-evident. The Jews and the Turks are scandalized by the horrible wickedness of these three religions. Not even with gallows and torture can they keep them, who are of one faith, from murdering one another in their homes, which happens often enough. What is still more horrible, they go publicly to war, and slaughter one another by the thousands. All this is the fruit of infant baptism.

No Baptist will be found in war, and few in prison or on the gallows because of their crimes. The majority of them are inclined to peacefulness. It is still possible to sleep unconcernedly among them and not need to fear robbery or even murder if one has much money. It would indeed be desirable that the whole world were full of these "deteriorated" Baptists. Their outcome has turned out far better than that of many from among the Pietists who have again taken an evil turn. Hardly had they left the great Babel several years before than they voluntarily returned to it. When the beginning is like this, the outcome will be very miserable and wretched. May God keep all Baptists in His grace so that they may not turn toward evil once more and then their outcome will be as mentioned above, namely, the eternal life of joy.

[GRUBER]

These are the most urgent questions about your new baptism and church, that were deemed necessary to present at this time to you, dear friends, for our own sake as well as that of others. You may now consider them, and prepare your corporate, clear, and candid explanations with your accompanying reasons. You should do this in such a manner as you can dare to account for such an important matter before the countenance of Jesus Christ, all His holy angels, and the elect on the inevitable day of most strict examination of this, your new work, without contradicting His noble Spirit in your consciences or those of others.

[MACK]

Beloved Friends:

Upon your request, we have published in love these answers to every one of the forty points of the searching questions which you have submitted to us upon our good consciences before God. They are answered according to our faith and good conscience before the God who sent His Son out of love to the world that we should hear, believe, and have eternal life through our faith in Him. If, then, your salvation and blessedness are dear to you, hasten and bow your necks under the scepter of this great King. Believe that His teaching is true and His baptism is saving and blessed for poor sinners. Do not say, "Of what use is this water for me?" and do not try to comfort yourselves with your infant baptism, which was introduced into the world in contradiction to God's Word.

Otherwise, may this simple testimony (which is published by the Baptists at Schwarzenau upon urgent appeal) be a witness along with your own consciences, at the great Day of Judgment of the Lord Jesus, who will come with flaming fire to take vengeance on those who were disobedient to His gospel. Now, to the strangled Lamb, who alone has might and power in heaven and on earth, be praise, honor, and glory, from eternity to eternity. Amen.

"Behold, he is coming with the clouds, and every eye will see him, every one who pierced him" [Revelation 1:7]. Amen.

Published at Schwarzenau, in the month of July, in the year of our Lord 1713.

Rights and Ordinances

Mack's largest book, titled *Brief and Simple Exposition of the Outward but Yet Sacred Rights and Ordinances of the House of God . . .* , was first published in 1715, likely by the same printer in Berleburg. It is set in the form of a conversation between a father and son. The second printing of this book was by Christopher Saur in 1774, along with the earlier Basic Questions. Other printings and translations soon followed.

A Brief
and Simple
Exposition
of the Outward but Yet Sacred
RIGHTS AND ORDINANCES
of the
House of God
as the True Householder
Commanded and Bequeathed
in Writing in His Testament;
Presented
in a Conversation
Between Father and Son
in
Question and Answer
by
ALEXANDER MACK
One also Called to the
Great Supper.
1715

- -
Psalm 119:126
"It is time for the Lord to act, for thy law has been
broken."
Verse 130
"The unfolding of thy words give light; it imparts
understanding to the simple."

[PREFACE]
Dear Reader!

God is a deity who is almighty and omnipotent; He is and
always has been very wrathful to all those who are disobedient to Him. He very severely punished the disobedience
of the first man in Paradise. Later He severely punished even
His own people for their disobedience under the Law:
whoever trespassed against the Law of Moses was put to
death without mercy, on the evidence of two or three
persons. Yes, God sent word to His people through Moses,
His servant (Deuteronomy 4[:1, 2]): "And now, O Israel, give
heed to the statutes and the ordinances which I teach you,
and do them; that you may live, and go in and take posses-
sion of the land which the Lord, the God of your fathers, gives
you. You shall not add to the word which I command you,
nor take from it; that you may keep the commandments of
the Lord your God which I command you."

It can be seen here how strictly God commanded that
what He had spoken to His people through His servant Moses
must be kept. Thus, it may be readily believed that God most
certainly wants everything to be kept which He has made
known and revealed to the whole world in these latter times
through His beloved Son. That is, all who call themselves
Christians should live as children of one household. The
good Householder [*Haus-Vater*] has given them rules and
laws which they are to keep and respect well and prudently.
Along with it, He has promised them life eternal, if they will
obey Him in all things—insignificant as well as important
ones. However, none of the teachings and ordinances of our
Lord Jesus may be considered insignificant, for they were
indeed commanded and ordained by an all-powerful
Monarch and King. Because of the greatness of the
Sovereign, even water baptism—which was commanded by
Jesus to be performed in His name—must also be considered

important, as well as all of His other commandments.

Just as the Ruler of the New Covenant is great, so are His statutes and laws truly great as are the promises which He added to them. These are life eternal, and all of the other gifts of grace of the Holy Spirit which believers possess. Likewise, the punishment of those who deny the gospel of Jesus Christ will be unfailingly harsh and most terrible. Paul says in the second letter to the Thessalonians in the first chapter [verse 8] that the Son of God will come with "flaming fire, inflicting vengeance upon those who do not know God and upon those who do not obey the gospel of our Lord Jesus." Yes, it is testified in the Revelation of John in the twenty-second chapter, verses eighteen and nineteen: ". . . if any one takes away from the words of the book of this prophecy (wherewith the teaching of Jesus is especially referred to), God will take away his share in the book of life. . . . If any one adds to them, God will add to him the plagues described in the book."

Therefore, we felt moved out of love to call to the attention of the kind reader the true and lawful use of the things which Christ commanded the members of His household to do, and also, to some extent, the great abuses which have prevailed among all of the Christian parties. We want to leave it up to the judgment of each one to examine this. It will be presented in the form of a dialog between a father and his son, who are journeying as travel companions.

A Conversation Between Father and Son in Question and Answer.

SON: Dear father, as we are all by ourselves in this wilderness, I shall tell you what happened to me in a certain company when I was not with you. I was criticized because of our baptism, and was called an Anabaptist, for we rebaptize those who were already baptized as infants. I was also severely criticized by those who, although they were baptized as adults but only by aspersion, are despite this baptized by us if they desire to join our church fellowship. I was criticized as well about the Lord's Supper and the ban, that we were legalistic about feet-washing, and also because of our using unleavened bread at communion. I was so attacked by all kinds of rational arguments that I could not give an adequate defense of our principles. Therefore, I am asking you, dear father, that you might better instruct me in accordance with the witness of the Holy Scriptures and the early Christians in all these things which are yet so controversial and which cause us such criticism. In this way, my faith will be confirmed and I shall be able to give to other people an accounting truly based on the Scriptures. In return for this, I shall show my gratitude to you for the rest of my life.

FATHER: Dear son, I shall give you ample instruction concerning this in as simple and satisfactory a manner as I can. Therefore, be sure to listen carefully, and ask me about those things which you were unable to answer, so that we can have a single-minded conversation.

[ON WATER BAPTISM]

SON: Beloved father, I am happy that you are willing to instruct me. I shall now diligently ask you and listen [to your replies]. Tell me then, where in Holy Scripture is outward water baptism founded?

FATHER: The eternal and almighty God is the actual founder of water baptism. As early as Noah's time, He began to reveal a prefiguration [*Vorbild*] of the water baptism of the New Covenant. Since men very quickly became wicked, the Lord God sent a flood, and these godless men were drowned in the water. The Apostle Peter said of this (1 Peter 3:20, 21): "Baptism, which corresponds to this, now saves you, not as a removal of dirt from the body but as an appeal to God for a clear conscience, through the resurrection of Jesus Christ." Yes, note further, when the Lord God wanted to make a prefiguration through His servant Moses as a testimony which should be revealed through the Son (Hebrews 3), Moses had to be lifted from the water by the daughter of Pharaoh. For that reason she also stated that "she named him Moses, for she said, 'Because I drew him out of the water' " (Exodus 2[:10]).

When God with a mighty hand led the seed of Abraham out of Egypt by this same Moses, and they were delivered from the Egyptians, this escape took place through the sea, which is a strong prefiguration of the baptism of the New Covenant. Paul calls it a baptism: ". . . all were baptized into Moses in the cloud and in the sea" (1 Corinthians 10:2). Again, as the Lord God had a tabernacle erected by Moses, which was a prefiguration of the household or church of the Lord Jesus, Moses had to make a large laver or vessel before the tabernacle where the priest Aaron and his sons were to wash themselves first before they could go into the tabernacle (Exodus 30:18-20; 40:12). This was also a strong prefiguration for the water baptism which was commanded by Jesus: no one can enter or be in the Lord's church without first being baptized in water upon confession of faith in Jesus.

Yes, you can see further how the Lord God commanded in the Law that when a leper was cleansed from his illness he had to wash his body in water (Leviticus 14:8, 9). Likewise, when the women wished to purify themselves, they had to bathe or wash in water. Again, various kinds of water baptisms were commanded by the Law, which all pointed to the water baptism of the New Testament.

Now, I will also tell you about the nature of water baptism in the New Covenant. Note well. When God the Father wished to reveal His dear Son in the world, there had to be a forerunner, namely John [the Baptist], who came into the land of Judea by divine command. He preached that men must repent, and also baptized them in water for repentance, that they should believe in Him who was to come after him—that is, in Jesus, the Son of God. He baptized at Aenon near Salim, because there was much water there.

SON: Oh, was there not great excitement among the people because John did such an extraordinary act as baptizing people in water?

FATHER: At that time, water baptism was not a strange act among the Jews, as it had already been common previously under the Law for outward cleansing. Therefore, there was no great surprise concerning the baptism as such, but in regard to his preaching the baptism was a new thing to them. He called upon men to repent and spoke of the Son of God that He would come, and called upon people to believe in Him.

SON: Did the theologians and the people in high places also submit to being baptized?

FATHER: Oh, no! The act was contemptible in their sight. They "rejected the purpose of God for themselves, not having been baptized by him," which can be read in Luke 7:30. However, Jesus, the Son of God, obeyed His Father in this, because He knew that John's baptism was from heaven. Therefore, He went quite a distance from Galilee to John at the Jordan and was baptized (Matthew 3:13).

SON: That was indeed a great miracle, and a [sign of] great humility by the Lord Jesus, that He permitted himself to be baptized in water by His servant, John.

FATHER: Yes, indeed! It was a great miracle and a great self-humiliation of the Son of God. He has left this to us and all of His followers as a mighty example in which we should follow Him.

SON: Was Jesus baptized merely so that we should follow Him on that point?

FATHER: The Son of God knew well the plan and will of His Father. For this reason He said to John, "For thus it is fitting for us to fulfill all righteousness" [Matthew 3:15]. The Son of God wished to found and ordain a water bath for His entire church, that it should be an efficacious seal and outward symbol of all those who would believe in Him. Thus, the Son of God, in the first place, fulfilled the will of His Father (because the baptism by John was commanded by God), and at the same time made a beginning of water baptism. This was no longer to be a baptism for repentance, but rather a baptism for those who had already repented and who believed in Jesus Christ, the Son of God. They were to be baptized upon their faith and confession, in the name of the Father, the Son, and the Holy Spirit.

When the Lord Jesus was baptized and came out of the water, a voice was heard from heaven which said: "This is my beloved Son, with whom I am well pleased" [Matthew 3:17]. The Holy Spirit came as a dove above the Lord Jesus. Therefore, this inception of the water baptism of the New Testament certainly had a mighty founder and author, namely, God the Father, God the Son, and God the Holy Spirit. The Lord Jesus also commanded that baptism should be performed in these three most exalted names.

SON: After Jesus was baptized, did He then immediately begin to teach and practice water baptism?

FATHER: Yes, the Lord Jesus immediately began to make disciples and to baptize them. You can read this in John 3:26; 4:1. The disciples of John came to him and said: "Rabbi, he who was with you beyond the Jordan, to whom you bore witness, here he is, baptizing, and all are going to him." John answered: "He must increase, but I must decrease. He who comes from above is above all. . . . He bears witness to what he has seen and heard, yet no one receives his testimony; he who receives his testimony sets his seal to this, that God is true." Yes, John also testifies in his first letter (5:6) that the Son of God came with water and blood and with the Holy Spirit, and that these were the three witnesses on earth.

SON: Does one also find that Christ commanded water baptism after His resurrection?

FATHER: Yes, I will explain this to you. In the first place, when the Lord Jesus wished to send the disciples out into all the world to preach His gospel, He gave them a specific commandment that they were to teach and baptize in His name all those who believed in Him (Matthew 28:19, 20), "teaching them to observe all that I have commanded you. . . ." You can see this further from Acts 2:37, 38; when the people asked what they should do, Peter answered: "Repent, and be baptized every one of you in the name of Jesus Christ for the forgiveness of your sins; and you shall receive the gift of the Holy Spirit"

SON: Can one read elsewhere of others who baptized?

FATHER: Yes, in Acts 8:5-12 it states that Philip preached at Samaria about Christ, and those who believed were baptized, both men and women.

SON: Oh, father, it says here: "They were baptized, both men and women." Were there no children baptized then?

FATHER: Oh, no! There is not a single example of that in the New Testament. Rather, the apostles baptized only those who publicly confessed their faith in Jesus through true repentance. Jesus, their Master, commanded them only that those were to be baptized who could be taught before and after baptism.

SON: Did not Christ command that children be baptized, and did not the apostle do that?

FATHER: Christ commanded only to baptize believers, and certainly not the children.

SON: Oh, but does it not say in Matthew 19[:14] that Christ speaks: "Let the children come to me, and do not hinder them; for to such belongs the kingdom of heaven"?

FATHER: Notice well that it adds, "And he laid his hands on them, and blessed them [and went away]." It says nothing about baptism.

SON: I have also heard it said that the apostles baptized entire households, among whom there must have been children.

FATHER: Only reason says that children must have been among them. The Holy Scriptures do not say a single word about it.

SON: Water baptism is indeed an important commandment as you have shown me from the Old and the New Testament. However, if a child dies before it is baptized, does it not suffer the loss of its salvation by dying without baptism? Many say that baptism was introduced instead of circumcision; when a male infant was not circumcised on the eighth day, it had to be killed.

FATHER: I am glad you asked that. Note well the plan and intent of God at all times. Whenever God commanded something, He wanted it to be kept just as He commanded it. The circumcision of the Old Testament was demanded only of male infants on the eight day. If then, a child had died before that time, he would not have violated God's commandment. Doubtless many died before the eighth day, and they were certainly not rejected, as little as the female infants, who were not circumcised at all, and despite this were under the promise.

Therefore, if a child dies without water baptism, that will not be disadvantageous for it, because this has not been commanded of the child. It has not yet experienced the "eighth day"—that is, the day on which it could have repented and believed in the Lord Jesus, and could have been baptized upon this, its faith. This was the point of the eighth day with circumcision. That is the reason why baptism is commanded only of adults and believers, and not at all of children. The children are in a state of grace because of the merit of Jesus Christ, and they will be saved out of grace. On such important matters of faith there must be specific commandments.

SON: Does one not find in histories that the early Christians baptized their children?

FATHER: We find in Gottfried Arnold's *Portrayal of the First Christians* that infant baptism began to be practiced only at the end of the second century after Christ's birth. At first, they did it only upon request for those who desired it. Later, baptism was only at Easter. Finally, a certain pope issued an order that no child should die without being baptized. Thus, it has prevailed through long-continued custom until everyone now thinks that infant baptism was commanded by Christ.

SON: You have already told me much about water baptism and its importance. Now, I would like to ask whether there is something special about water, because God commanded so many cleansings in water in the Old Testament, and again in the New Testament he ordained and founded water baptism for His believers.

FATHER: Observe well. Water is an element created by God. All things are created through water; yes, the entire earth subsists of water and is based upon it. Man himself is born in water in his mother's womb. Indeed, the Spirit of God first moved upon the waters, and therefore there is in water a divine mercy. Christ also sanctified water by His baptism. For this reason he has spoken (John 3[5]): "Unless one is born of water and the Spirit, he cannot enter the Kingdom of God."

Nevertheless, believers do not look to the power of water in baptism, but rather they look to the power of the word which has commanded it. Christ ordained a water bath for His church and wished to cleanse them by the water bath in the Word, as Paul says (Ephesians 5:26). The faithful, therefore, believe that obedience to the commandment of water baptism cleanses them and frees them from future punishment. This is true only if the person does not let himself sink again into filth by sinning and violating the Word after this washing. God looks only upon obedience, and believers are bound to obey the Word. Then they will achieve eternal life by obedience.

SON: If a person denied himself everything—gave his goods to the poor, prayed and fasted much, but did not wish to be baptized because it was an outward act—could not such a person please God?

FATHER: Note well. If a person did these things out of true faith and love of God, they would be good and saving things. Such a person would certainly not refuse to submit himself willingly to this commandment of water baptism. "For this is the love of God that we keep his commandments. And his commandments are not burdensome" (1 John 5:3).

Moreover, Paul says (1 Corinthians 13:3): "If I give away all that I have, and if I deliver my body to be burned, but have not love, I gain nothing." He then describes the way of love as believing everything that God has commanded. Yes, Christ says (John 14:23, 24): "If a man loves me, he will keep my word. . . . He who does not love me does not keep my words. . . ."

Therefore, a man may indeed do much by his own sanctity, and despite this, still not hold to the love of Jesus as the Head. There were people like this in Paul's time. He writes in his letter to the Colossians (2:18) about those who go about in "worship of angels." Paul says that they have "a sensuous mind" (verse 19), because they did not rely on the Head.

SON: Cannot then a man love God despite this, even if he does not want to obey in just one point, but performs all of the rest?

FATHER: Are you not yet able to realize what James says (2:10): "For whoever keeps the whole law but fails in one point has become guilty of all of it" [?] Think about it yourself. If you had been obedient in everything to me for ten or even more years, and I requested you to pick up a piece of straw, and you did not want to do it and did not do it, I would have to consider you a disobedient child. Even if you said a thousand times, "Father, I will do everything; I will work hard; I will go wherever you send me, but it does not seem necessary to me to pickup the piece of straw because it neither helps you nor me," I would say to you, "You are a disobedient wretch."

SON: Father, you say this about yourself, but is God who is love similarly minded toward His children? If so, how can this be proved?

FATHER: I will prove it to you very clearly from the Holy Scriptures that God is so minded. Just consider what the first man in Paradise did. God said to him that he should eat from all of the trees except one, from which he was not to eat. Behold, as soon as he ate of the forbidden tree, he lost all of his happiness and was expelled from Paradise for his disobedience. Yes, consider further what God did and commanded in the Law (Numbers 15:30, 31): "But the person who does anything with a high hand . . . because he has despised the word of the Lord, and has broken his commandments, that person shall be utterly cut off."

Again, when the sons of Aaron brought unholy fire before the Lord, they suffered death (Leviticus 10:12). King Saul was rejected because of his disobedience to the Lord (1 Samuel 15:22, 23). Similarly, Achan and his entire family had to die because he disobeyed the commandment of God in that he took some of the prohibited spoils, which was forbidden by God, at the taking of the city of Jericho (Joshua 7:20). Yes, it would be possible to cite many more similar testimonies from Holy Scripture, but these are sufficient. You can see from them that God demands absolute obedience from all of His creatures.

SON: I well perceive that man should not only heed that which is commanded, but also the Master himself, and especially His greatness. Therefore, all of the commandments of the great God shall be esteemed great.

FATHER: *Yes, that has always been the true faith and the true love of all saints and believers. They have done what God has commanded them to do, and have bowed all of their reason and will before the will of their God. It can be heard or noticed of no believer that he has ever rebelled against a single commandment of God.*

SON: If then so much, indeed, everything depends upon the keeping of God's commandments, why is it that God has always commanded men to do but simple things, as can be seen in the Old and New Testaments?

FATHER: Notice well, God is himself a simple and good Being, and does not need the service of men. He has many thousand times a thousand angels and spirits who serve Him. The commandments which God has always given men are for their sake, so that men shall become truly lowly and simple through them. Man rose to great heights through the fall of Adam and wants to be great, mighty, and holy in his own sight. In order to redeem man from his perilous condition, God ordered through His Son that [certain] simple things be done. If man does them in true faith and in obedience holds his reason captive, he will gradually become single-minded and childlike. It is just in this single-mindedness that the soul again finds rest, peace, and security. Therefore, Christ says: "Truly, I say unto you, unless you turn and become like children, you will never enter the kingdom of heaven" [Matthew 18:3].

SON: I now well understand that all commandments point only to true obedience. The same is true of water baptism, which Christ commanded His apostles to perform, and which they then did. Was this commandment given to all believers that they should be baptized, and is this comm-mandment to remain until the end of the world?

FATHER: This is very clearly expressed in Matthew 28:19, 20, where our Savior says "Go therefore and make disciples of all nations, baptizing them (etc.) . . . teaching them to observe all that I have commanded you; and lo, I am with you always, to the close of the age."

SON: After the death of the apostles, were other men allowed to baptize who had not been sent to do this as were the apostles?

FATHER: Mark well the household plan and ordinances of God already under the Law: When God had a house built by Moses in which the priests were to serve, the tribe of Levi was chosen for this by God. From this tribe, God himself elected Aaron and his sons as the ones who were to carry out the offices of priests. Whenever the temple and everything else was destroyed and ruined, and they again wished to observe their worship services, no other than someone from the tribe of Levi could conduct it. However, the godless King Jeroboam appointed people as priest who were not from the tribe of Levi. They could also perform idol worship (1 Kings 12:31). But when they chose priests from the tribe of Levi, they appointed those who were well versed in the Law of Moses. They dared not have blemishes or infirmities of the body (Leviticus 21).

Therefore, note this well that it was the Son of God himself who established in His church first of all apostles, and later teachers and others like them. The apostles soon chose others in the service of the household of God to baptize, to administer the ban and the like, so that the divine ordi-nances might be well maintained. However, at all times they chose only those who were decended from the royal priesthood, that is, those who had the Spirit of Jesus. They were permitted to baptize, and to do other things by this same Spirit. Now, the apostles had already in their time noticed men who were indeed Christians in appearance, but did not have the Spirit of Christ. Paul apeaks of them to the elders in Ephesus (Acts 20:29, 30): "And from among your own selves will arise men speaking perverse things, to draw away the disciples after them."

This has always been a characteristic of the false spirits: whenever a person seeks honor for himself, he is not of the manner of Christ, who had not placed himself in the priesthood, but rather was placed by His Father. It can be seen in Acts 20:18-28, that the first teachers and elders of the churches were appointed by the Holy Spirit. The apostle Paul had the elders and teachers of the church of Ephesus called to him, and he gave them this admonition, among others, "Take heed to yourselves and to all of the flock, in which the Holy Spirit has made you guardians, to feed the church of the Lord which he obtained with his own blood."

When, however, men appointed themselves to the service of the church by their own spirit and their own honor, the great abuse and every evil originated and spread. There are many thousand preachers in the world, but only a handful have the royal priesthood of the holy nation (1 Peter 2:9). Only a handful have the Spirit of Christ. Only a handful were appointed bishops by the Holy Spirit. It is for that reason that they preach only for their own honor and profit.

On the other hand, after the death of the apostles the faithful church which remained pure and undefiled always chose men from among them who had the Spirit of Jesus and denied themselves. Just as Christ chose His apostles outwardly, so has the church of the Lord (as the body of Christ) in turn chosen those whom they recognized as capable. These have then also baptized. The commandment of the Lord Jesus in its purity has never been lacking nor ceased, as He says (Matthew 28:20): ". . . teaching them to observe all that I have commanded you." Rather, this command will remain until Christ comes again to judge His own servants and also His enemies on His teaching.

Cyprian and other devout men of the early church required of a person who wished to baptize, a true and sound belief in Christ, and proper appointment thereto by his church. The Council at Ilibris likewise wrote and demanded of one who wished and was to baptize that he must be correctly baptized himself, and not have fallen again from grace by sinning after his baptism. Gregory also reports: "Consider each worthy and capable enough to administer the office of baptism if he can be counted among the godly."

SON: I understand now very well about baptism, that it is a command from Christ to His believers until the end of the world. Now, I would like to know for certain about the mode of baptism. Should one baptize in water, or can baptism also be performed in a room with a handful of water and still fulfill the act of obedience of the commandment?

FATHER: Note well; I will explain this to you from the Holy Scriptures. In the first place, Christ, the true forerunner of His entire church, was baptized by John in the Jordan (Matthew 2[3]:13, 16). John baptized at a place near Salim, because there was much water there (John 3:23). You should be able to see sufficiently from these two testimonies that if the commandment of baptism could have been fulfilled on dry land, John would not have gone where there was so much water. It is indeed much more convenient to baptize in a room than in the water, because the water is often cold and tends to weaken the constitution.

For good measure, I will tell you of yet other testimonies. The Greek word for the command *to baptize* actually means to immerse. It is so translated by most translators.[1] However, since the practice of aspersion [sprinkling] has developed, and the theologians have shied away from the water because of their frailty, they maintained that the Greek word can also be taken to mean to asperse, to pour, or to make wet. Nevertheless, they have to admit that it means to immerse. Further, when Philip baptized the eunuch, it states: ". . . and they both went down into the water, Philip and the eunuch, and he baptized him" (Acts 8:38, 39). Much can be found in the histories about the early Christians baptizing in rivers and streams and wells.

In addition, it can be seen in the *Martyrs Mirror* [*Bloedig Tooneel . . .*] of the Mennonites (page 265), that in 980 A.D. many persons were baptized in the River Euphrates. It further states (page 207) that Paulinianus [Paulinus] baptized at noon in the River Trentha [Trent] near the city of Truvolsinga in the year 1620 [620]. It is written there that this baptism was called by the ancients an immersion or dipping [*Unterdomplung*]. It further states (page 220) that the English were baptized in the Rivers Schwalbe and Rhine, and that it could not be done in any other way or manner. Yes, people must be quite blind and prejudiced, because this is written so clearly even in the Holy Scriptures. In Romans

6:5 it is called a burial of sins. Paul further calls it a water bath (Ephesians 5:26). Christ says (John 3:5) that one must be "born of water and of the spirit.

The early Christians spoke thus of baptism: "The carnal children of Adam (they said) enter the water, and after they have become spiritual children of God must rise from the water." Justinian gave this account of it to the emperor himself: "Those who are converted and believe that what we teach is true, and who also promise that they wish to live in this way through the grace of God, are taught how they are to pray, fast, and seek forgiveness for their sins from God. After this, we lead them to a place where there is water, and they are reborn, just as we were reborn; they are cleansed in the water in the name of God the Father and the Lord of all things, and of our Lord Jesus Christ, and of the Holy Spirit." The above-mentioned Justinian said to Caesar: "We have received this manner from the apostles."

Bede (book 2, chapter 14) also testifies that from time to time at the beginning of the first congregations the English people were immersed in rivers. Wallfried Strabo writes in his book, *On Ecclesiastical Matters* [*De rebus eccles.*] (chapter 26), that it should be made known that the believers originally were baptized in flowing waters or wells. Our Lord Jesus himself was baptized by John in the Jordan so that He would sanctify this bath for us, as can be read: "John also was baptizing at Aenon near Salim, because there was much water there" (John 3:23).

Yes, Nicodemus testfies in his description of the crucifixion of the Lord Jesus that after the Lord Jesus' resurrection many saints rose [from the dead] and appeared in Jerusalem and testified that Jesus had risen. Among those risen were the two sons of the old Simeon who had taken the Lord Jesus in his arms in the temple and praised God. They, namely Karinus and Lentzius, testified that the Lord Jesus had also awakened them, and that the archangel Michael had commanded them to go along the Jordan to a lovely place where many others were who had also risen. They were baptized in the river of Jordan, and received exceedingly bright robes as white as snow.

Further, the above-mentioned Nicodemus testified that the Emperor Tiberius, during whose reign the Lord suffered, sent a great prince named Wolusin to Jerusalem to bring

the Lord Jesus to him to heal him, because he had heard
that He could do that. When, however, the prince arrived
in Jerusalem and learned of the deeds and teachings of the
Lord Jesus and that Pilate had crucified Him, he had Pilate
put in chains, and then he returned to the emperor. He told
him everything and also said that Jesus wanted all who
believed in Him also to believe in being immersed three times
in water and baptized. Upon this, the emperor said: "Woe
is me, that I was not worthy of seeing Jesus myself." He had
Pilate placed in prison, where he committed suicide out of
desperation.[2]

SON: It seems to me that you have shown me sufficient
testimonies to prove that Christ, John, the apostles, and very
many of the early Christians were baptized in water.

FATHER: That would, of course, be adequate, but I wish
to refer you to even more testimonies from the histories of
the early Christians. Hononus Aug. [Honorius
Augustodunensis] writes in his book, *The Soul's Jewel*
[*Gemma animae*] (book 3, page 106): "It should be known
that the holy apostles and their disciples used to baptize
in flowing waters and wells." Tertullian reports in his book,
On the Chaplet [*De corona militis*]: "Those who are to be
baptized profess some time previously in the church before
the teachers that they renounce the devil, his pomp and
angels; after this, they are immersed three times and
baptized. This custom was maintained until 801, and the
time when Ludovicus [Leo V] was made emperor in 815."[3]

SON: Do tell me also whether the apostles immersed the
entire person or just a hand or the head, or how was it done?
I have heard many say that it can be clearly seen from Scripture that one should go into the water, but how the baptism
is to take place is not certain.

FATHER: You reveal with this question that you lack inner light. Those who say that it is not known how baptism
should be performed reveal that they have a miserable
teacher. Is it possible that Jesus is the kind of a teacher who
requires His own to do something in His name, such as an
act as important as baptism, and would not let it be known
in what manner it is to be done? [If that were so] they would
have to ask the teacher how they should do it, and better
refrain from it than perform it in uncertainty. Just consider
that those men want to be the stewards over the mysteries

of the House of God, and do not even know how one should baptize in water. Where, or from which teacher, did they learn that they could sprinkle the head with a handful of water or make it wet, in a dry place in a room or meeting place? This cannot be found in one single place in Holy Scripture and the exact opposite can be seen from Jesus and His apostles.

Since you have asked me about this, I will explain it briefly. You have heard about Christ and His apostles, and many testimonies of the early Christians, that they baptized in flowing waters and wells, and that baptism is nothing else but immersion. This is as the Word and the commandment require, for Christ said to His apostles (Matthew 28:19): "Go therefore and make disciples of all nations (mankind), baptizing them (immersing them)," and not [baptizing] the bells, such as happens under the papacy. The Lord Jesus did indeed not say to baptize the head or some other part of the body of the person, or sprinkle the person a little with water in His name. No, the Lord Jesus did not command this, but rather that the whole person should be immersed in water. As I have already told you about the significance of the baptism, it must have inner significance.

SON: Cannot the water bath or burial of sins be symbolized by a handful of water or the like?

FATHER: That is impossible, for that which should symbolize an outward thing cannot be different from what it is essentially.

SON: Would it really matter if the essence were inward, and its outward symbol were different from the inward substance?

FATHER: Note well. Suppose a great lord should say to his servant (who wished to be a painter) that he should make a portrait of him so that others could see and recognize the lord who do not see him physically. And suppose that the servant, when he did this, did not pay strict attention to his lord, but rather his mind was occupied with other things—he did not really love his lord, but nevertheless wanted to fulfill the command—and he painted his lord with great carelessness. Further suppose that he painted him without one eye, or one foot or one hand, and the protrait was therefore completely distorted, so that there was absolutely no resemblance with the subject. What should the lord then say to a servant like that? He would dismiss him from his service as a worthless servant.

There are unfortunately many such worthless painters in the world, especially where water baptism and all of the other commandments of Christ are concerned. The hearts of most of them are filled with the love of the world and of self. As the love of Jesus the crucified and the love of denying themselves is not in them, they have also forgotten the image of Jesus in His teaching and His mighty example. They have, therefore, completely distorted the teaching of Jesus. Each one paints as he wishes according to his own will, or as it is customary here and there. They do not look singly and alone to their Lord and Master. Some sprinkle small children a bit on the head. Others, who approach it somewhat closer, sprinkle adults with a handful of water on the head; some take three handfuls, others but one handful of water. All say, "I baptize you." This is supposed to be a water bath or a burial of sins.

SON: I perceive clearly that the teaching of Jesus is very much distorted, and that no accurate image of it can now be seen or felt.

FATHER: Yes, a great darkness now covers all of the people and the entire world. However, it will be soon illuminated again, as is prophesied (Zechariah 14:7; Revelation 18:1).

[ON THE LORD'S SUPPER]

SON: I thank you, dear father, that you have told me all this. I am very much astonished about the great abuses concerning baptism in these times. There must have indeed been great darkness covering the nations. I must, however, ask you now something else, concerning the Lord's Supper. How was it instituted by Christ? How should it be held? Is this also in a state of decay as is baptism?

FATHER: You can well assume that if people err so much in one thing, they will err in all others too. You will see this clearly from the ordinance of Christ and the present custom. In the first place, it is called a supper which the Son of God established as a memorial for His beloved disciples. He commanded that they should thereby proclaim His death on the cross, break the bread of communion, drink the cup of communion, and covenant with one another in love as members of Christ to be ever more faithful to their Lord and Master. Further, that they should remain steadfast with Him in true obedience of faith even to the cross, so that they may partake of the great Supper with Him at the end of the world.

SON: Are only the true followers of the Lord Jesus, who keep His commandments and help to bear His cross, permitted and intended to partake of the Lord's Supper, or should and may others partake of it?

FATHER: The true Householder, Jesus Christ, commanded this only of the members of His household who have entered the Kingdom through true repentance and faith and baptism, and who willingly keep all of the rules of the Householder in obedience of faith. The Lord God commanded under the Law that whoever wished to keep the Passover of the Lord must first be circumcised (Exodus 12:48). Therefore, whoever wants to keep the Lord's Supper worthily must first be separated from the body of Satan, the world, yes, from all unrighteousness, and from all false sects and religions. he must cling to Jesus the Head as a true member in faith and in love. He must be ready to give his body, and even life, unto death, if it is demanded of him, for the sake of Jesus and His teachings according to the will of God in the evanglical manner. Whoever still lives knowingly in sin and disobedience toward God, and will not follow Christ in the denial of self and all things of the world according to the counsel of Jesus in Luke 14:26, 27, is still unworthy. "For any one who eats and drinks without discerning the body eats and drinks judgment upon himself" (1 Corinthians 11:29).

SON: Oh, father, how does it then happen that it is called a Lord's Supper and despite this it is usually held in the mornings or at noon and not in the evening?

FATHER: Just as I told you above about baptism, that it has fallen into great decay and disorder, so it is with the Lord's Supper. Some hold it in the morning, others, at noon but none have it as a supper. When an evening or a noon meal is to be held, there must be something to eat! But here the people go to their so-called "supper" and return from it hungry and thirsty. Some do not even receive a bit of bread and a little wine, but at the same time are filled with great extravagance of clothes, sensual debauchery, selfish pride, and the like. This can be seen in the great parties in all religions, when they claim to keep the Lord's Supper.

SON: Must it then be held in the evening and must there

be a real meal with it, or is it not also good to hold it without the other meal in the morning or at noon?

FATHER: Observe well, that the true believers and lovers of the Lord Jesus have always looked steadfastly and single-mindedly to their Lord and Master in all things. They follow Him gladly in all of His commands, just as He has told them to do, and as He has shown them by His own example. they thus learn in their simplicity to understand well the intention of their Master, even in the simplest matters. In the first place, it says in the Scriptures, a "supper" (1 Corinthians 11:20). The believers observed it that way, having learned it from Paul this way, as is stated in the same chapter (verse 1). Paul in turn, had himself received from the Lord Jesus that which he gave to the Corinthians (verse 23). They thus held an evening meal or a supper.

Now, blind reason can (if it but wanted!) indeed recognize and make the differentiation that an evening meal could not mean a noon meal. As early as Paul's time the people came together and held the supper. But Paul says (1 Corinthians 11:20) that they did not [really] hold the Lord's Supper. When, however, the believers gathered in united love and fellowship and had a supper, observing thereby the commandments of the Lord Jesus that they wash one another's feet after the example and order of the Master (John 13:14, 15), yes, when they broke the bread of communion, drank the chalice (the cup) of communion, proclaimed the death and suffering of Jesus, praised and glorified His great love for them, and exhorted one another to bear the cross and endure suffering, to follow after their Lord and Master, to remain true to all of His commandments, to resist earnestly all sins, to love one another truly, and to lie together in peace and unity—that alone could be called the Lord's Supper.

They can then rejoice and comfort themselves in the suffering of the Lord Jesus. By such a supper they portray that they are members and house companions of the Lord Jesus. They will one day observe the Great Supper with the Lord Jesus at the close of the world and enjoy eternal happiness.

Paul says about this above-mentioned supper that "any one who eats and drinks without discerning the body eats and drinks judgment upon himself" [1 Corinthians 11:29]. When, however, people eat a morning or noon meal, who have not truly repented, who do not believe in the commandments of the Lord Jesus, who are not baptized upon true repentance and true faith, who still love the world, the lust of the eye, the lust of the flesh, and the pride of life, who live in envy, hate, gluttony, drunkenness, and the like—that is not the Lord's Supper. Rather, it is a custom which has been introduced by reason and by the worldly spirit through the wrongly praised artfulness of the theologians in their many rational conclusions; through long habit it has become fixed in the simple people. Everyone now thinks that he goes to the Lord's Supper, but in reality it is not what he thinks it is.

SON: Can obvious sinners be permitted at the Lord's Supper?

FATHER: Obvious sinners cannot be permitted at the Lord's Supper, even if but one work of the flesh is evident in them (about which Paul writes in Galatians 5), if repentance or improvement does not take place after admonishment. Moreover, not only do they not belong at the Lord's Supper; they do not even belong in the Kingdom of God, and do not belong in the church of the Lord. Just as they are excluded from the Kingdom of God because of their sins, so must they also be excluded from the church of the Lord.

[ON SEPARATION]

SON: Oh, father, I thought that each person must give an account for himself alone. What damage does it do if my fellow member has something evil in him, when I myself am devout? If despite this, I told him in love that he should abstain from his sin, and he did not want to, I could still treat him with love and remain in fellowship with him. He would have to give an account for himself.

FATHER: Listen and observe well! This idea has a very good appearance of love, but it is only a feigned love and is absolutely unlike the manner of God's love. Divine love cannot be minded other than God [is]. Yes, it cannot love other than that which God, who is eternal love, has commanded and ordained. It cannot believe other than that which God has commanded to believe. The true divine love cannot and may not prescribe to the Spirit of God in meaning, wisdom, and counsel. The true love of God looks only to God, its eternal source. The person in whom the love of God really exists looks to and learns from God about His character and nature.

Now then, a true child of God (because of the exclusion mentioned above) has learned from his heavenly Father at all times a division and separation—namely, that between the pure and the impure, between light and darkness, between His people and the Gentiles. This can well be seen in the creation; when God created heaven and earth there was light and darkness, earth and water all intermingled; then God separated the light from the darkness, and called the light day and the darkness night. Further, when God planted a Paradise, and created out of love all kinds of delightful things, He also created out of love man in His own image. He made him so worthy that he was allowed to live in Paradise and even eat of the fruits of Paradise which God had offered to him. As soon, however, as man became disobedient to his God, he became unclean, and as an impure being could not any longer remain in Paradise. He had to leave, until he was cleansed by Christ (the second Adam); then he could re-enter Paradise. Adam had to wait many hundred years, until Christ, the promised seed of woman, led him back into Paradise. Along with Adam, many other saints rose after the resurrection of the Lord Jesus, and He led them all with Him into His Kingdom. This can be seen in Matthew 27:52. Here may be seen how sin and disobedience separate us from God and His Kingdom.

Again, God revealed to Abraham, the father of all of the faithful, about a separation and division in respect to circumcision. This was that his seed should be a people separate from the heathen. He thus led them with a mighty hand from Egypt, and pledged to give them a promised land. The Lord God gave His people a special Law upon the Mountain Sinai in the desert, whereby they should be completely separated—not only from the unclean heathen, but also from the unclean animals, fish, and birds. God said to them (Leviticus 20:24-26): "I am the Lord your God, who have separated you from the peoples. You shall therefore make a distinction between the clean beast and the unclean, and between the unclean bird and the clean; you shall not make yourselves abominable by beast or by bird or by anything with which the ground teems, which I have set apart for you to hold unclean. You shall be holy to me; for I the Lord am holy, and have separated you from the peoples, that you should be mine."

You thus see how God has herein revealed His plan and will in the separation of the clean from the unclean, the Lord's people from the heathen (who were indeed also God's creatures, but were not granted any part of fellowship with the people of God).

SON: Yes, dear father, I have understood clearly from you about the separation among the people of God in the Old Testament with the Levitical priesthood, which taught such outward ceremonies. However, Jesus Christ fulfilled the Law as an eternal High Priest and did not promise an outwawrd Canaan but proclaimed an eternal Kingdom which is spiritual. Therefore all of His laws are spiritual. How, then, does one understand the separation in the New Testament, or is separation necessary? I would like to be thoroughly instructed about this.

FATHER: Note well, and pay close attention to the Word of the Lord Jesus and His apostles. You will thus recognize an inevitably necessary separation in the New Covenant between believers and unbelievers. The Lord Jesus says (Matthew 13:24) that the present world is like a field in which good and bad seeds are planted. The Lord Jesus sows the good seed through His gospel; these represent the children of His Kingdom who are brought forth by the Word of Truth (James 1:18). The weeds, however, are the bad seeds, the seed of the devil, planted by him through his false, cunning, and lying word so agreeable to human wisdom. Now the harvest from these seeds is the end of the world. At that time the Lord of the Harvest will gather the good seeds into His barn, but He will burn the bad seed with everlasting fire.

Now, notice well, as is mentioned above, that the separation in the Old Testament was commanded through Moses, which was all spoken by the servant Moses as a testimony toward the Son and His household (Hebrews 3:5, 6). There no uncircumcised, no lepers, no one who had made himself unclean by touching a corpse, was permitted to enter the temple. In like manner Jesus, the Son of God, instituted and ordained a temple, a church, and a houshold by His death on the cross and by His Holy Spirit. In the Holy Scriptures this temple or church is called the body of the Lord Jesus (Romans 12:5; 1 Corinthians 12:27; Ephesians 1:22, 23; 4:12; 5:30; Colossians 1:18). All members of Jesus are planted and baptized into this holy temple or church. Paul says (1 Corinthians 12:13): "For by one Spirit we were all baptized into one body."

This body, temple, or church (which is all one) is cleansed by Jesus as the Head by the "washing of water with the word" (Ephesians 5:26). This body or church is separated from the world, from sin, from all error, yes, from the entire old house of Adam—that is, according to the inner part in faith. This church is named in the Holy Scriptures a "chosen race, a royal priesthood, a holy nation" etc. (1 Peter 2:9), because this body, according to Romans 6:2-4, is dead to sin and is buried by baptism into death and is risen again to a newness of life in Christ Jesus; it remains and lives in it as a fruitful wine. However, this body or the church of Christ still walks outwardly in a state of humiliation in this wicked world. It thus happens through divine permission that Satan is allowed to tempt each member with sins, with various errors, and all kinds of wicked and harmful deeds day and night, in order to test his faith and love. Therefore, the Lord Jesus and the apostles call upon the faithful to watch and pray, struggle and strive.

Nonetheless, it can easily happen that one of these members, who once died to sin and put on the Lord Jesus in the newness of life, sins again, perhaps against one of his fellow members or even against the ways and statutes of the Lord, if he does not remain constant in prayer and watching. In this case, the Lord Jesus teaches, as the true Head of His body (Matthew 18:15): "If your brother sins against you, go and tell him his fault, between you and him alone. If he listens to you, you have gained your brother. But if he does not listen, take one or two others along with you, that every word may be confirmed by the evidence of two or three witnesses. If he refuses to listen to them, tell it to the church; and if he refuses to listen even to the church, let him be to you as a Gentile and a tax collector."

Behold, you can see who is the founder of the separation and the ban in the New Testament, namely, the Lord Jesus, the true Householder. This is then a separation of those sinners whose sins can be forgiven without their being disowned, when the sinner is willing to hear. If he will not hear, he is not excluded because of the sin, but rather because of his hardness of heart and arrogant pride. He rejects the counsel of the Spirit of God, and grieves and despises the church even though he is obligated to die for his fellow members rather than grieving them and despising their good counsel.

The Law has already spoken of such wicked men (Numbers 19: 13): "Whoever touches a dead person . . . (which is a slight matter in itself) and does not cleanse himself, defiles the tabernacle of the Lord, and that person shall be cut off from Israel," etc. That which is the water of aspersion in the Old Testament by which the unclean were cleansed is the brotherly discipline in the New Covenant. If then, a member sins, and does dead works of sin and despises the brotherly discipline, the deceitfulness of sin has already hardened that heart. Paul warns (Hebrews 3:13) the believers to take care that "none of you may be hardened by the deceitfulness of sin. For we share in Christ, if only we hold our first confidence firm to the end." That is, we have become partakers in the new life from Christ Jesus. Let us also remain steadfast therein until the end, and by no means abandon again the true life in Christ and the living God by the old life of sin.

SON: If then a man can be excluded from the body and church of the Lord and even from the eternal Kingdom of God because of a minor sin (which could be easily forgiven if he listened), what will then happen if a member knowingly commits a premeditated sin, a lie or the like, or even fights against the statues and law of the Lord?

FATHER: Note well the mind of the Spirit of God in all things. He is the best counselor (knowing everything beforehand), and has therefore arranged everything wisely in His household. God already commanded under the Law (Numbers 15:27-30) that if a person or an entire congregation sins unknowingly against a commandment of the Lord, they are to bring a sacrifice to the Lord and the sin shall be forgiven. When, however, a person sins against the commandment and ordinances of the Lord out of wickedness, there is no sacrifice for this, but such a person shall be cut off, and his iniquity shall be upon him because he has despised the word of the Lord and has broken His commandment. Yes, if an entire congregation or city should sin like that, and serve other gods—that is, do those things which the Lord God has forbidden—that entire city should be destroyed (Deuteronomy 13:12).

Now see how this must be observed in the church of the Lord according to the spirit of the New Testament, so that the gates of hell, which are sin, may not prevail against it. Now, each member of the body of Jesus knows full well that he was buried into death through baptism (Romans 6[:4]) and that he should walk in newness of life. At the time of his baptism he was also charged that he must renounce completely all sins and the devil, along with his own will, and that he must obediently follow after the Lord Jesus, being steadfast in all suffering, until death. Now, the works of the flesh are indeed plain according to the witness of Galatians 5:19. They are: adultery, immorality, licentiousness, impurity, idolatry, sorcery, enmity, strife, envy, anger, contention, dissension, partisan spirit, hatred, murder, drunkenness, gluttony, and the like. If a single one of these evils becomes manifest in a member, to all such the Kingdom of God is completely denied by the Holy Spirit.

If then, a work like this is evident in a member of the body of the Lord, so that the church can clearly recognize it, then it is only just that such a member be expelled from the church according to 1 Corinthians 5:13, until he is cleansed of it by true penitence and repentance. This is so that the entire body or church is not contaminated by it. How wicked and corrupt must then a member like this be, if he wishes to justify himself in doing the works of the flesh.

[ON DISSENSION]

SON: I well see herein the plan of God. But this work of "dissension"—I cannot rightly recognize what that is. I would like to know it.

FATHER: This is the kind of spirit which those persons who are not sufficiently enlightened encounter on the paths of the Lord, just as Eve met the serpent in Paradise. It said: "You will not die. For God knows that when you eat of it [the forbidden fruit] your eyes will be opened, and you will be like God, knowing good and evil" [Genesis 3:4, 5]. This then also took place in part; namely, as soon as they had eaten, the eyes of both were opened, and they saw that they were naked. Therefore, Paul says to the Corinthians, "I am afraid that as the serpent deceived Eve by his cunning, your thoughts will be led astray from a sincere and pure devotion to Christ" (2 Corinthians 11:3).

As long, then, as a faithful member of Christ remains in this conflict, and he "destroys arguments and every proud obstacle to the knowledge of God and takes every thought captive to obey Christ" (2 Corinthians 10:5)—so long will the carnal spirit of dissension be unable to capture his soul. Rather, the member walks in simplicity, in obedience of faith, in peace, and in unity with his fellow members. He willingly leaves in peace and in simplicity to his fellow members that which he does not understand. He humbly submits himself to his fellow members, after the counsel of Peter (1 Peter 5:5).

As soon, however, as this spirit—that is, the spirit of dissension—becomes master of those who do not know it, the person is slowly but surely separated inwardly from peace and love toward his fellow members. He takes offense, now against this, then against that, and gradually loses the true power of faith. The meetings of his fellow members, where he should rightly be edified, will also become burdensome for him. If this is noticed, and he is asked about it in love, then he can more readily listen to frivolous and trifling conversation than to the loving admonitions of his fellow members, who notice and recognize this. If the person refuses to listen to the loving exhortations of his fellow members, but rather listens to the false and deceitful spirit which disguises itself as an angel of light, he will be made to think himself so clever and wise that he sees with keen eyes all of the faults of his fellow members, is repelled and offended by them, and afterwards begins to censure them as well as the entire congregation.

This person eventually opposed the whole congregation. This kind of spirit of dissension always works through such a member to bring about the separation of all other members to abolish all order and to be his own master. He usually wins a following. This is called by the Spirit of God dissension and party-spirit; it is plainly a work of the flesh. It does not belong in the Kingdom of God, nor in the church of the Lord, but rather in the old house and kingdom of Adam, which is complete division and therefore will not endure. It must fall because division has always been the origin of all evil. No earthly household can endure in blessing where there is dissension, much less a divine household.

Therefore, true believers must avoid all such spirits within themselves and also all such persons must be avoided outwardly who create scandal and division in this and other ways, as Paul admonishes (Romans 16:17). Those are works of the flesh and a carnal spirit, and that is a carnal person, even though he disguises himself outwardly in angelic humility. Paul also calls and refers to such people in this way (Colossians 2:18). Yes, he even calls it "heresy, which should be avoided (Titus 3:10).

[ON THE BAN]

SON: I have clearly understood about the spirit of dissension, and about those who should be avoided. But, dear father, I ask you to tell me what kind of person it must be who conducts and administers this ordinance of the ban. We all have many faults and fall short of the glory of God. James says, "If any one makes no mistakes in what he says he is a perfect man" [3:2]. Since, then, we all lack faith, who is it that should avoid others because of their shortcomings or sins?

FATHER: It is very good that you ask me about everything so that you do not remain ignorant on any point, for ignorance causes great damage to the soul. Take notice, then, and pay attention. In the first place, no other people are promised salvation except the faithful, who believe in the Son of God. They shall have eternal life. Those who do not believe shall remain under the wrath of God. Now note this manner and quality of faith, as Jesus the Son of God has described it (Mark 16:17). The Lord Jesus says there to His disciples: "And these signs will accompany those who believe: in my name (that is, in His teaching, word, and commandments) they will cast out demons; they will speak in new tongues; they will pick up serpents, and if they drink any deadly thing, it will not hurt them; they will lay their hands on the sick; and they will recover."

These believers are promised eternal life, and these believers are commanded by Christ to reject the sinful, offensive, self-seeking spirits, to exclude them from their fellowship. Whatever these believers bind on earth, that will be certainly also bound in heaven; what they loose on earth, that will also be loosed in heaven. These believers put into effect the royal statutes and ordinances of His house and walk amid much temptation with great joyfulness of faith, according to the rule of their Lord and Master, even when they are rejected by men for this as evildoers. Even though these faithful members of Jesus may unwittingly also make mistakes and commit sins, they do not do it intentionally, but rather are truly sorry for it in their hearts. They are the kind who suffer because of their weakness. When they are corrected by their fellow members, they listen very willingly, and allow themselves to be told where they have fallen short. They are those of whom John speaks: "My little children . . . if any one does sin, we have an advocate with the Father, Jesus Christ, the righteous" (1 John 2:1). They stand in an unrelenting battle and war within themselves and by continually doing so mortify the sinful members of earth. Yes, they would rather be outside of the church of the Lord than that they should sin and not desist when they are disciplined.

These believers can then with good conscience also help to exclude and avoid even their beloved fellow members when the latter sin and will not listen to loving admonition. This is possible because they have in themselves already rejected and banned such a mind and spirit. These believers can also say with assurance of faith that which John says (1 John 4:6): "We are of God. Whoever knows God listens to us, and he who is not of God does not listen to us. By this we know the spirit of truth and the spirit of error." These believers then can with a good conscience exclude from their midst a member who no longer will permit himself to be disciplined and edified in love. When a member sins and no longer listens, then this is a mortal sin and is one which cannot be prayed about, as John records (1 John 5:16).

Thus, you see the great difference in sinning. Two men can commit the same sin: one may be lost and the other may attain mercy. You can see this in the two criminals who were crucified with Jesus. The one went with Jesus to Paradise because he confessed his sin and believed in the Lord Jesus. It can likewise be the same in a church that two members commit the same sin. One listens and is sorry for his sin, and will be forgiven. The other will not listen to the discipline of love and sits in arrogance and selfishness, and will be lost. Therefore there is a great difference in sins. David says: "Blessed is the man to whom the Lord imputes no iniquity, and in whose spirit there is no deceit" (Psalm 32:2). These are the upright souls who are regretful when they, perhaps, were overhasty and made mistakes. They listen, however, very willingly to the admonition of love from their fellow members. James says about them: " . . . we all make many mistakes" (James 3:2).

Nevertheless, they are in Christ Jesus, and there is "therefore now no condemnation for those who are in Christ Jesus" (Romans 8:1). They "walk not according to the flesh, but according to the Spirit" (verse 4). They cannot sin to condemnation, for they are born of God, and God's seed keeps them (1 John 3:9). These are the blessed seeds of woman who are in daily combat against sin, which is the seed of the devil. There is continual enmity between believers and the seed of the serpent. They must also feel its bruises on their heels, although its head—that is, its dominion—has been crushed and removed. Therefore, the faithful are called the church militant as long as they live in a state of humiliation. They "have conquered him by the blood of the Lamb" (Revelation 12:11).

SON: I now understand somewhat about the difference between sinners, as well as about avoidance and its causes. However, I have heard many say after they had been banned that they felt perfectly well. They did not feel any ban. I have also heard from others that the ban had neither power nor effect, because those who are placed under it do not feel it, but say that they are in good spirits.

FATHER: Note also here the mind of God, and you will easily see how such poor souls who know neither themselves nor God are deceived by the slyness of the serpent. When they first repent of their sins, and believe in the teachings of Jesus, they enter by faith into the church and the divine ordinances. They themselves help to conduct the ban for a time, and believe that whatever the church of the Lord binds on earth, that will also be bound in heaven. However, such poor souls do not want to "contend for the faith" according to the counsel of the Apostle Jude (verse 3), but rather abandon the faith again. They incline in their hearts toward seductive spirits, whom they look upon as good angels, as Paul clearly writes about (1 Timothy 4:1). They listen to those spirits who promise them nothing but good things, and complete freedom, as also the Apostle Peter wrote about (2 Peter 2:18, 19).

If, then, these poor souls abandon the faith, their consciences are branded as with a hot iron. But, because they have left the faith they do not feel the ban until the day of revelation. Yes, they can speak proudly to the church of the Lord: "You can ban me as you will; I shall still come into grace with God." The others, however, who are banned because of their sins, and have not abandoned the faith, indeed feel the ban. They repent, and are restored again through faith.

Now consider well the great blindness of these people who find fault with a church because some if its members who have abandoned it say, as mentioned above, that they feel no ban, but rather can still contend against the church of the Lord. Now note that God himself conducts a ban like this with the majority of mankind. All unreborn men lie under the wrath of God. His eternal damnation awaits them if they do not truly repent and are reborn to Jesus through belief and live according to the will of God. Now, look at these men. They are merry and cheerful, and have within them a hope of salvation, which has been planted there by the false gospel. They are the kind of people about whom Jesus speaks (Matthew 24:38, 39) as they were in the day before the flood: ". . . they were eating, and drinking . . . ," etc. They were happy until the flood came and swept them all away. They let Noah preach and build his ark; they even mocked him and did not believe.

It will be exactly like this with mankind when the coming of the Son of man shall be revealed. They will not believe that their condition is so bad, and, therefore, they will not feel the divine ban within themselves, although it already rests upon them. Unbelief has hardened their hearts and made them stubborn, like Lot's wife, who turned into a solid pillar of salt. Likewise, the poor souls who once departed from the sinful Sodom and who looked back on their way became pillars of salt who no longer believe the gospel. The Apostle Peter says: "For it would have been better for them never to have known the way of righteousness than after knowing it to turn back from the holy commandment delivered to them" (2 Peter 2:21). Therefore, the Lord Jesus calls to His followers with a strong voice, "Remember Lot's wife" (Luke 17:32).

Consider further the angels who sinned. God "cast them into hell and comitted them to pits of nether gloom to be kept until the judgment" (2 Peter 2:4). See how these angels conducted themselves. They again fought against the good angels, which can be seen in the letter of Jude (Verse 9) and in Revelation (12:7). Notice, the strife with Satan and with the Lord Jesus himself (Matthew 4). In such a case, these poor and blind men could also say to God that His ban had no effect. If the angels banned by God could still fight against the good angels, do not be surprised that the banned people, who have abandoned the faith and follow such banned spirits, can still contend against the faithful and cause them much trouble. This is, however, only for the increasing of their damnation, and to test the faith of the believers and increase their salvation.

Therefore, do not be concerned about what other men say, for in most cases their testimony is false and goes against the mind of God. Even though the testimony of such men is accepted, the divine testimony is still much greater (John 5). God has testified about His Son; whoever believes in the Son of God has the divine witness in him, which is more certain than all of man's testimonies, no matter how it appears. Here you have heard sufficiently the reason and the cause of those who are banned and their manner of contending against the church of God.

SON: If then a church conducts a ban and separation for itself, would the civil authorities permit this?

FATHER: Mark well, that this good ordinance is not opposed to the authorities, but, on the contrary, is conducive to the station of civil government. The faithful are taught by Paul (Romans 13:1-7) that they should be subject to the human regulations made by the authorities for the sake of the Lord, who instituted them. They should give the government taxes, imposts, honor, and respect, for all authorities are ordained of God to punish the evil, and to help to protect the good, provide that they desire to carry out their offices in accordance with the will of God. The authorities should rightly rejoice if they had only those subjects who walk in the fear of God by not permitting any evident sinners within their communion, and who willingly, in the fear of God, give the authorities what is owed them and who give the Lord, their God, that which belongs to Him. The Lord has foretold such a time [in which] the kings will be the wet-nurses of the church of the Lord (Isaiah 60:16).

[ON OATH-TAKING]

SON: Will the government also be satisfied if one does not swear the oath, according to the teaching of Christ?

FATHER: If the true believers affirm with "Yes" what is "Yes" and deny with "No" what is "No" in accordance with the teaching of Christ, that is much better than many oaths which are mostly sworn and not kept. Therefore, the government can feel much more secure and more sure of the truth with those subjects who tell them truthfully "Yes" and "No" in the fear of God and remain in the truth than with those who swear the oath and are still not to be trusted or believed.

[ON EXAMINATION]

SON: Dear father, I thank you that you have instructed me upon all of these points. I perceive well that to have a sure foundation in sacred things, it is necessary to look to God. He has revealed himself in His Word at all times and remains steadfast in faithfulness, and thus the heart is made firm through grace. I want to ask you something else which I also heard said, and about which I would like to be certain. Why are people not tested prior to their baptism and acceptance into the church, rather than first being baptized and then being put into the ban? They claimed that this shows that the spirit of examination is not present which is certainly necessary for this work.

FATHER: Dear son, listen and remember again herein how people still do not recognize and understand the divine mind and way. Because of this they judge and reject a thing which they do not understand according to human opinions. I will also clearly explain this so that you can understand or grasp it well. In the first place, the faithful dare not be of a different mind in the household of God than God has revealed himself to be in His household. They dare not wish to be more wise than God. Even if they should all be looked down upon by men as fools, they must despite this still abide with divine wisdom. Therefore Paul speaks: "If any one among you thinks that he is wise in this age, let him become a fool that he may become wise. For the wisdom of the world is folly with God" (1 Corinthians 3:18, 19).

Now, since the believers must look only to God in all things, it is but just that they look to God in the testing of men. Now, one cannot see and learn from God any other way than this: when He wished to test a man or a people He first laid His laws and commandments upon this man or the entire people. Only then were they really tested under His laws and commandments. This has been the manner of divine wisdom at all times and still is (Ecclesiastes 4:19; 6:22). That this is true can be seen, in the first place, in that Adam did not have to be tried outside of Paradise, but rather within it. He was under the will of God to see whether or not he would eat the fruit which God had forbidden him to eat. Secondly, Noah had to be tested in his faith in the construction of the ark, and in his entering into it.

Again, Abraham, the father of all the faithful, was severely tested in that God ordered him to go out from his own country and from his friends. The most difficult test occurred for him after he had already received the covenant of circumcision, when he was to sacrifice his son Isaac (Genesis 12:1; 22:1). Again, it can be seen that God severely tested the entire seed of Abraham in Egypt, and also after they had been led with a mighty hand from Egypt. Then God began to tempt them and test them in the wilderness. Although they had already received God's pledge of the promised land, they were first tested in the wilderness, so that it would be revealed what was in their hearts—whether they would keep God's commandments or not. This can be seen in Deuteronomy 8:2.

In this wilderness of temptation, most of them were struck down because of their disbelief (unfaithfulness). God had no pleasure in them. Although they were already baptized in the cloud and in the sea under Moses, and all of them had eaten the same food—even angel food, as the Book of Wisdom calls it (Wisdom of Solomon 16:20). Yes, they had "all eaten the same supernatural food, and all drank the same supernatural drink. For they drank from the supernatural Rock which followed them, and the Rock was Christ" (1 Corinthians 10:3, 4). They did not stand the test, when God demanded obedience for his evidenced love and favors and toward His commands, ordinances, and laws.

Now, see and observe the intent of God in the New Covenant. In the first place, we read that there was no examination before the baptism of the Son of God. However, when he was baptized by John in the Jordan, and the voice was heard from heaven [saying], "This is my beloved Son, with whom I am well pleased" (Matthew 3:16, 17), then temptation began. It was then that the devil tempted Him, that the scribes and the Pharisees tempted Him, that He had to learn obedience (Hebrews 5:8). He was obedient unto death, even death on a cross (Philippines 2:8).

In the same manner and in no way as the Father led and tempted the Lord Jesus, the Son of God, does Jesus lead His followers. "The kingdom of heaven is like a net which was thrown into the sea and gathered fish of every kind . . . but [the men] threw away the bad" (Matthew 13:47, 48). The Lord Jesus called a great many who became His disciples by faith and baptism (John 4:1). However, they were then tested and made elect by the cross in His faith. The Lord Jesus never examined men except for His teaching and gospel, but rather all those who came to Him and believed in Him were accepted as disciples. He said to them: "If you continue in my word, you are truly my disciples, and you will know the truth, and the truth will make you free" (John 8:31, 32).

Again, the dear Jesus said to His disciples: "He who abides in me, and I in him, he it is that bears much fruit, for apart from me you can do nothing. If a man does not abide in me, he is cast forth as a branch and withers" (John 15:4-6). The church of the Lord Jesus must have this mind and no other. If a man repents and publicly renounces the devil, the world, and all sins, and desires to enter the teaching of the Lord Jesus, and supposing that it could be suspected that perhaps this man would not remain steadfast but nothing evil were known about him at that moment, then this man could not, upon his public profession, be excluded from the church, The man will first be tested by the discipleship of Christ; then it will be revealed whether he rejects the teaching of Jesus, which is the true stone of examination.

This is attested by [the Book of] Wisdom (Ecclesiasticus 6:22 [21]. Divine wisdom invites all men to come to it, yes, even the fools (Proverbs 9:1-4). It excludes no man who accepts the invitation, forsakes the path of folly, and takes the path of wisdom. Man is tested afterwards in the household of God, when he must put his feet into the fetters and his neck into the yoke (Ecclesiasticus 6:25 [24]. If he then does not remain loyal, then the guilt is upon him alone.

This is the divine intention that man, after he has entered

into a relationship with his God, is only then tested in the commandments of God. Otherwise, God himself could be blamed for instances in the Old Testament, that He had not been able to test the men who accepted His promises but did not remain steadfast. Yes, even Jesus Christ could be accused that He accepted men who did not remain true to Him. Why did He not make as His disciples only those who remained true to Him? It states: "After this, many of his disciples drew back, and no longer went about with him" (John 6:66). All of the apostles could be accused in the same way. It can be seen from their letters that they made many disciples by their preaching of the gospel, and at all times many turned away again in all kinds of manner and ways.

Now, notice well this simple comparison; if two persons love each other and decide to marry, when can they really test each other? Before marriage they are still free of the burdens of the household, the woman is still free from obedience to the man, and he is still free from the cares and weaknesses of the woman—all they know is love. As soon, however, as they enter into a public marriage relationship, and begin a household, then begins the real test. Then the wife dare not flirt with any other man, for she must be obedient to her husband. Then the husband becomes aware of the weakness of the wife, and the like. The first passionate love is dissipated and a divine love is required if they are to live together in peace. Then a love is necessary which must be steadfast until death. They must share joy and sorrow, the sweet and the bitter, and cleave to each other until death. That is the state of marriage among the faithful, which symbolized the Lord Jesus and His church (Ephesians 5:32).

When worldly people desire to marry and have not decided upon anyone, they commonly are first inclined to the one and then to the other, and are completely fickle. They find fault with the married people and think that they will live much better when they are married. When, however, they are actually married, then they must first learn how to run a household, and many become adulterers. They do not have enough love and patience to endure in the testing period.

Notice well what happens similarly in the spiritual realm. How many souls have been awakened and have forsaken the great harlot—have gone out of the great outward Babel—and have fallen in illicit love in various ways with the teachings of Jesus? One takes here a verse of the [New] Testament, and another takes there a verse, and with these they make love illicitly. They also pretend great love for one another, call one another "brethren" and "sisters" and are also able to live in this love. They are, however, not joined or baptized into one body through one Spirit (1 Corinthians 12:13). Therefore, they have freedom among themselves for each to indulge where and how he will. One inclines to this opinion, the other to that. The one holds to this spirit, the other to that. All this time they remain together in this illicit love. Yes, it is said among them, "Love covers all, and condemns none."

It is true that this uninhibited illicit love covers all, for it is not a marriage with Christ and His church to walk according to His rules, in which there is no room for illicit love, but rather a love which hates all that is evil, wicked and sinful, if it is not to be false (Romans 13:9). These lovers may be judged and criticized by those who have entered into the marriage with Christ and have committed themselves, who edify one another, work, and admonish. It may happen that among them one inclines to a different spirit and illicitly loves it, so that they judge this person an adulterer and exclude him from the church if he will not listen. Then this person goes at once to the company of illicit lovers, where he can illicitly love all of the false spirits outside the house and church of the Lord. That is then called a great liberty of the spirit, and it is indeed so, but it is also outside of the house of God, outside of His church, and outside of His Kingdom.

In the Kingdom of God there is no disorder and no false freedom, but it is all order and unity. All of the angels and spirits in heaven must will what God wills or they cannot remain in His Kingdom. As soon as the angels desired something different from [what] God [willed], they were ejected and bound with the chains of darkness to be kept until the judgment (2 Peter 2:4). This is the nature of the true love of God, and therefore all believers must be minded as their Lord and Master has taught them. He has also portrayed it in this understanding, namely, if one of the members of your body "causes you to sin, cut it off and throw it from you" (Matthew 8[18:8]). Jesus has given this commandment especially to His church, which is His body, to cut off all sinful and offensive members, lest the entire body be spoiled. This love was commanded by God already under the Law: ". . . [if] your friend who is as your own soul, entices you secretly, saying, 'Let us go and serve other gods,' which neither you nor your fathers have known . . . you shall not yield to him or listen to him, nor shall your eye pity him" (Deuteronomy 13:6). The illicit lovers know nothing of this kind of love, as long as they do not enter the state of marriage with Christ in His teachings and ordinances.

Nevertheless, they pride themselves greatly on their unpartisan love which they have and pretend. They are also considered by uninitiated souls to be men who walk in a great divine love and in good faith. It will be revealed that this was only a false, illicit love, which was indeed well disguised by eloquent and clever speeches, by which many innocent hearts have been deceived. Therefore, say the Scriptures: "Let love be genuine" (Romans 12[:9]). The essence of the commandment is ". . . love that issues from a pure heart and a good conscience and sincere faith. Certain persons by swerving from this have wandered away into vain discussion . . . " (1 Timothy 1:5). Here you see that an adulterated faith and also an adulterated love can exist.

[ON LOVE AND FAITH]

SON: Yes, but how can we test the true love and the true faith, or the false love and the adulterated faith?

FATHER: The true faith which is genuine and which is promised eternal life must be a Scriptural faith, just as the Lord Jesus says: "He who believes in me, as the Scripture has said, 'Out of his heart shall flow rivers of living water' "(John 7:38). Where there is a Scriptural faith, it will also produce the true love according to the Scriptures. "This is the love of God, that we keep his commandments" (1 John 5:3). The Lord Jesus says of the true love: "He who has my commandments and keeps them, he it is who loves me; and he who loves me will be loved by my Father, and I will love and manifest myself to him" (John 14:21). By this Scriptural love His disciples will be known (John 13:34, 35). Just as the Lord Jesus was born in accordance with the Scriptures and crucified and resurrected in accordance with the Scriptures (1 Corinthians 15:3, 4), so He taught all of His own a Scriptural faith and promised them eternal life in accordance with the Scriptures. But an adulterated faith and an adulterated love cannot be founded on Scripture, but rather only on human opinion.

The one believes that which he was taught by the theologians, the other as he was convinced by this or that book, the third, according to his own mind's opinion and self-will. But the Scripture says specifically: "There is [but] . . . one Lord, one faith, one baptism" (Ephesians 4:5). If there were ten men who were still standing in an adulterated faith, and if they were to be examined in accordance with Scripture, it would be learned that each of the ten had his peculiar faith, and not one of them would be completely in accord with the Scriptures. There is only one single unadulterated faith, and all those who have true faith according to Scripture are also unified according to Scripture as far as the rules of faith are concerned.

[ON THE SCRIPTURES]

SON: I have, however, heard it said that all sects appeal to Scripture, and therefore one cannot prove one's faith with Scripture.

FATHER: Whoever says that because all sects appeal to Scripture a true believer dare not do so must really be a miserable and ignorant person. Rather, it greatly strengthens the faith of a believer to know that all sects recognize the Holy Scriptures as divine and appeal to them, even though they do not believe. To appeal to Scripture and to believe in Scripture are two vastly different things. This can well be seen from the words of the Lord Jesus, who said to the Jews: "If you believe Moses you would believe me, for he wrote of me" (John 5:46). Now, the Jews had all referred to Moses, but they had not believed in his writings. Likewise, all of the sects are based not only on the Scriptures, but also on the Lord Jesus himself. However, the way they believe in the Lord Jesus is the way they believe in the Scriptures. Now, if a true believer were so blind as to think or say: "Oh, all sects appeal to the same crucified Savior, therefore I may and can not appeal to Him," that would certainly please the devil. But no! The true believers have learned more and better wisdom from their Lord and Master.

When the devil appealed to Scripture during the temptation of the Lord Jesus, Jesus answered in faith from the Scriptures and referred to them (Matthew 4:6, 7). Let the devil and all false spirits appeal to Scripture; they do not really believe it. You will learn that the very people who try to confuse a believer by saying that all sects appeal to Scripture will nevertheless appeal to it themselves. Therefore, a faithful child of God looks only to his heavenly Father, and believes and follows Him in His revealed Word, because he is certain of and believes that God and His spoken Word are completely one. Otherwise a believer would have to abstain from many things, if he did not wish to do in faith that which the godless and unbelievers do in disbelief.

He would not dare to pray, sing, work, eat, sleep, and the rest, because these are all sin for the wicked and abominations before God. "To the pure all things are pure, but to the corrupt and unbelieving nothing is pure" (Titus 1:15). Therefore, learn well the true Scriptural distinction in all things, so that you do not become confused, as have, unfortunately, many souls in this day. They see that also the godless perform acts of worship such as prayer, singing, holding of meetings, baptizing, holding of the Lord's Supper, and the like. The unenlightened mind says: "If the godless do these things, they are not very important. They can be completely rejected." Such people become so confused in different ways that finally they do not know what they think or believe. They have to make a faith for themselves which is not taught by Scripture. They think that they have achieved more than the apostle. Moreover, they no longer take counsel from the writings of the apostles.

During my life I have known and heard many such people. I have also experienced that the outcome of their path has brought with it complete disaster, for they very quickly fell and perished so that they were destroyed. Finally, they did no longer believe in anything, but again fell victim to the world and the wide path. May God protect in grace all simple believers in Christ that they do not desire to climb so high, but "associate with the lowly" (Romans 12:16). Paul admonishes Timothy with these words: ". . . from childhood you have been acquainted with the sacred writings which are able to instruct you for salvation through faith in Christ Jesus. All scripture is inspired by God and profitable for teaching, for reproof, for correction, and for training in righteousness, that the man of God may be complete, equipped for every good work" (2 Timothy 3:15-17).

SON: Can and may we believe the witness of the Holy

Scripture in all things, and is a believer obligated to believe and follow the Scripture? Does not the Spirit of God lead him on other paths, of which the outward letter of the Scripture knows nothing?

FATHER: No one may say to a believer that he should and must believe and obey the Scriptures, because no one can be a believer without the Holy Spirit, who must create the belief. Now, the Scriptures are only an outward testimony of those things which were once taught and commanded by the Holy Spirit. The prophecies and warnings were also spoken through it. If, then, through true penitence and repentance, a person receives the Holy Spirit from God, the Father of all spirits, then it is the same spirit of faith which was present and worked in Peter, Paul, and John hundreds of years ago. True, the Holy Spirit was in the apostles in greater measure for the expansion of the gospel, yet it is the same Holy Spirit in all believers.

Whatever then Paul, Peter, and John wrote, ordained, and commanded at that time was all agreed to by all of the faithful of that time, insofar as they were still sound in the faith. Since there is one Spirit and only one, then this holy and unique Spirit cannot will other than that which He willed for salvation many hundred years ago. That which the Holy Spirit ordained for the faithful was written outwardly. All believers are united in it, for the Holy Spirit teaches them inwardly just as the Scriptures teach them outwardly. However, when men come to the Scriptures with their wisdom and carnal minds, they do not have the spirit of faith within themselves. Therefore, they cannot believe the testimony of the Scriptures outwardly, nor follow in obedience of faith. Indeed, it is not written for them, and therefore they are free from the commands which are contained therein.

This is just as if a king had commands written to his subjects, making great promises along with them if they followed his orders, and great threats if they did not keep them. Other people who are not subjects of that king are indeed able to read the commands and speak at great length about them. However, if they are not the kings subjects, nor wish to become subjects, they do not respect the threats and do not believe the promises. They do not submit themselves to his commandments, statutes and laws.

Exactly the same is true with the Holy Scriptures in the New Testament. Whoever reads it can see what Jesus, the King of all kings, has promised to all men who truly repent, believe in Him, and are willing to follow Him obediently in all of His commandments. He can also see and read in the Holy Scriptures with what the Lord Jesus threatens all unrepentant sinners who are not willing to repent and believe in His gospel, and who will not allow Jesus to reign over them by His Spirit through the commandments which He had left behind in written form. A man can indeed read the Scriptures outwardly and talk and write about them, but, if the spirit of faith is not in him, he will not be concerned with the commandments therein, nor be frightened very much by the threats which they contain. This is because the inner ears are not yet opened.

Therefore, the Lord Jesus said to the people who personally heard him preach: "He who has ears to hear, let him hear" (Matthew 11:15; 13:43). In the Holy Revelation of Saint John, the Spirit of God calls to each of the seven churches: "He who has an ear, let him hear what the Spirit says to the churches" (Revelation 2:7). Therefore, when a believing person whose inner ears are opened reads the Holy Scriptures outwardly, he will bear as the Lord Jesus intends His teaching to be understood. He hears that which the apostles want to express in their writings. He will also be impelled, through his inner hearing, to true obedience which makes him obey even in outward matters. Outwardly, he reads the Scriptures in faith and hears the inner word of life which gives him strength and power to follow Jesus. Where, however, faith is lacking, a person can indeed hear and read outwardly, and say: "It is a dead letter which I cannot follow. I am not inwardly convinced of what it states outwardly." He does not know, however, that he lacks faith, and the true divine love (John 14).

[ON THE OUTWARD AND INWARD WORD]

SON: I have, nevertheless, heard many say that the Christians stand in the New Covenant, and that the Law of God is written in their hearts. Consequently, they do not need to accommodate themselves to the outward Scriptues and follow them.

FATHER: I am glad that you have also asked me about this. Observe closely the true intention of God. You will easily realize that this talk contains some truth, but that it is also intermingled with lies. When, in times past, the Lord God revealed His Law to His people through Moses, God wrote the Law on two stone tablets. He gave them to Moses, who had to put them into the ark of the covenant (Deuteronomy 10:1-5; Hebrews 9:4). They had to make a copy of them and write them on the doorposts of their houses (Deuteronomy 6:6-9). There it states: "And these words which I command you this day shall be upon your heart; and you shall teach them diligently to your children . . . [And] you shall bind them as a sign upon your hand . . . . And you shall write them on the doorposts of your house . . .."

The outward copy was to be nothing else than, much less contrary to, that which God himself had written upon the stone tablets, and which lay hidden in the Holy of Holies in the ark of the Covenant. Therefore, the outward and the inward Law retained the same meaning. The Holy of Holies in the ark of the Covenant, in which the tablets of the Law lay, now corresponds in the New Covenant to the heart of each true believer. In it undoubtedly lie the tablets of the law of his God. They are written in each believer's heart, not by the hands of men, but rather by the Holy spirit. This law which is inwardly written by the Spirit of God is completely identical with that which is outwardly written in the New Testament. All of the latter had flowed from the inward, and is an express image of the inward living Word of God.

However, when a person says, out of haughtiness alone, that the laws of his God are written in his heart, while he opposes the orders, statutes, and laws which the Son of God and His apostles have ordained (of which the Scriptures testify outwardly) you may be quite sure that he is still of the world. The law which he claims to have in his heart was written by the spirit of errors and lies. Moreover, this is a clear indication of the law of God and the law of the deceiving spirit: all those on whose hearts the law of God is written are united in the one faith, the one baptism, and the one spirit in accordance with Jesus Christ. This is the perfect will of the true Law-giver that they who are His should be one even as the Father and the Son are one (John 17:12 [21]).

But the law which the spirit of error writes in hearts by its false gospel is of such a nature that it is, in the first place, completely uncertain about divine testimonies (Psalm 5:10).

Secondly, it separates men from God's commandments and ordinances, and divides men into manifold creeds and confessions. I have observed this of many who said that they were free men, that they did not need to subject themselves to the letter of the New Testament—meaning the written word—for the law of God was written in their hearts. But I have further seen and recognized that no two of them were agreed concerning the basic principles of the Christian life according to the Scriptures, but rather they had as many laws as there were persons maintaining such haughty opinions.

It has often occurred to me that this must be a foreign spirit which plants these various laws in the hearts of men. The Lord God complained about this already in the book of the prophet Jeremiah: the people of Israel, led astray by false prophets, abandoned the one Law of God and the one altar of the Lord. In their false freedom, they made other gods and altars as they thought best (Jeremiah 11:13). The same thing happens today with people of this time who boast of great freedom and do not follow divine counsel and commandments in accordance with Holy Scripture. Here is truly a case of "as many men—as many spirits and as many laws." Despite its great spiritual pretensions, Babel, confusion, and disunity remain. Even so, these builders will not refrain from their intentions, disregarding the fact that the Lord has confused their languages. Yes, they see that many learned and wise men have already built in this manner apart from the ordinances of the Lord Jesus, and have utterly failed, yes, some even made fools. Still, more builders begin once again to continue this chaotic construction. It becomes more and more confused and terrible. If they do not soon refrain from this, there will finally be "men of corrupt mind and counterfeit faith; but they will not get very far, for their folly will be plain to all, as was that of these two men [Jannes and Jambres]" (2 Timothy 3[:8, 9]).

Now then, you have learned about the true and the false laws which are both written in the hearts of men. The false law is written in the hearts of the unbelievers by the spirit of errors. The true law of life is written in the children of the New Covenant, the true believers, by the Holy Spirit of truth. It is in everyway identical with that which Christ commanded outwardly, and that which the apostles have written.

[ON BLOOD AND STRANGLED ANIMALS]

SON: I have now understood this sufficiently. It is very useful and necessary for me that I have been so well instructed in many things, because in this day keen eyes are needed to differentiate between and recognize the true and the false. Now I must ask you something else. I have read in Acts 15:29 that the apostles at Jerusalem forbade the believers among the Gentiles to eat blood and strangled [animals]. Must this still be observed?

FATHER: Note well that since blood in the Old Testament was for atonement, God said, as soon as He had permitted Noah and his sons to eat meat: ". . . you shall not eat flesh with its life, that is, its blood" (Genesis 9:4). God had this told to His people by Moses: "Moreover you shall eat no blood whatever, whether of fowl or of animal, in any of your dwellings. Whoever eats any blood, that person shall be cut off from his people" (Leviticus 7:26). God expressed this still more clearly when He said: "If any man of the house of Israel or of the strangers that sojourn among them eats any blood, I will set my face against that person who eats blood, and will cut him off from among his people. For the life of the flesh is in the blood; and I have given it for you upon the altar to make atonement for your souls; for it is the blood that makes atonement by reason of the life" (Leviticus 17:10-12).

There you see why God, in the Old Testament, forbade His people to eat blood. At the time of the apostles, those who had become believers from among the Jews had already learned from the Law not to eat blood. The believers from among the Gentiles, however knew nothing about it. Therefore, it pleased the Holy Spirit to command through the apostles as a necessary part that they refrain from eating blood, just as well as from unchastity (Acts 15:29). Since for the Christians the blood of the Son of God is their atonement, it is but right that they should eat no blood. It is also forbidden to do this in the New as well as in the Old Testament. The early Christian said to the Gentiles: "We are not so cruel as the beasts that when we eat the meat of animals we should also eat their blood and hunger for it." They placed the ban on those who ate blood, which can be seen in the *Portrayal of the First Christians* by Gottfried Arnold.

SON: I have heard stated, however, that the Lord Jesus said: ". . . there is nothing ouside a man which by going into him can defile him" (Mark 7:15). Further, that the apostle said: "Eat whatever is sold in the meat market . . ." (I Corinthians 10:25).

FATHER: The men who say this do not yet understand the unity of the Spirit. Rather, because they are disunited, they think that the Scriptures and the Spirit of God are likewise disunited—that in one place something is forbidden, yet in another place it is allowed. If Christ had meant forbidden things, one could drink to excess in good conscience, which is a great sin. And, if Paul permitted that everything might be purchased without discrimination which is offered to be sold at the meat market and eaten there are of course many things for sale which cannot be eaten at all. Just as little as Paul referred to other things than natural food that can be eaten, he did not refer to the buying and eating of blood. It remains, then, a settled point that the eating of blood and of strangled things is forbidden to all true Christians just as much as is unchastity by the Holy Spirit through the apostles.

[ON MARRIAGE]

SON: Tell me then, what is the place of marriage in the New Covenant? May believers marry, or how should marriage be practiced?

FATHER: The Lord God himself instituted marriage in Paradise, and the Lord Jesus himself said to the Pharisees: "Have you not read that he who made them from the beginning made them male and female, and said . . . the two shall become one?" [Matthew 19:4, 5]. Now, the state of marriage of two persons who are one in the fear of God and in faith in God is ordained and blessed by God himself. This can be seen in Abraham, Isaac, Jacob, and the other saints of the Old Testament. That the state of marriage is to be carried on in unity is already expressed under the Law. In the first place, the people of Israel were forbidden by God to marry outside of the descendants of Abraham (Deuteronomy 7:3). When the Lord God wanted to have His Law heard by the people of Israel, He had Moses tell them: "Be ready by the third day; do not go near a woman" (Exodus 19:15). Furthermore, God ordered under the Law that if a woman bore a female child, "she shall continue in the blood of her purifying for sixty-six days" (Leviticus 12:5); during this time there was to be complete continence. When a woman had her sickness, then continence was strictly commanded.

From all these commandments of God can be clearly seen that the state of marriage must be conducted in purity and in continence, and not in the plague of lust as do the heathen who do not know God. It may well be seen that God wanted the state of marriage in the Old Testament to be conducted in purity and continence. Now, under the New Testament, the state of marriage should and must be conducted not in a less holy, but rightly in a much holier manner. Paul said about unmarried persons that it would be good for them if they remained as he, Paul, was. If the unmarried state is conducted in purity of the Spirit and of the flesh in true faith in Jesus, and is kept in true humility, it is better and higher. It is also closer to the image of Christ to remain unmarried.

Nevertheless, if an unmarried person married, he commits no sin, provided it occurs in the Lord Jesus, and is performed in the true belief in Jesus Christ—that is, that they are one in true faith in Jesus Christ according to the teachings of Jesus and according to His commandments. This is what is meant by "The two shall become one," just as Christ and His church are one (Ephesians 5). There is no other way for a person to be one flesh of Christ and His members except when he accepts in faith the Word which was Jesus and that which He taught and follows Him in obedience. Then he is "bone of my bones and flesh of my flesh." This cannot be understood as the believers' corruptible flesh, for the flesh of Christ indeed cannot be corrupted. Therefore, the true state of marriage which God has instituted must consist of this unity, that they should be one not only after the outward and corruptible flesh, but that they must much rather be one in their hearts after the will of their God and of one faith in Christ Jesus. In no other manner is the state of marriage established or blessed by the Holy Spirit, than as here described.

When, however, people marry each other because of the lust of the eyes, lust of the flesh, and for the sake of wealth, and they do not take into consideration the unity of the faith in Christ—this marriage is cursed, and must rightly be rejected by true believers. Nor is it legitimate in the house or church of the Lord, and it has always been punished by

God. This may be seen in the instance when the "sons of God (fell away from God, became sensually minded, and they) saw the daughters of men were fair, and they took to wife such of them as they chose" [Genesis 6:2]. Then the flood had to come and kill them all. The Scripture calls those the children of God who were from the family of Seth, a son of Adam, and created in His likeness (Genesis 5:3). The children of man were, however, of the house of Cain, who was cursed by the Lord because of the murder of his brother. These two families were not to be intermingled, but they would not obey God, and so they all perished. But from the family of Seth, one seed was preserved, namely, Noah and his sons.

However, the devil soon succeeded in bringing Ham, that is the son of Noah, under the curse, so that his father Noah cursed him (Genesis 9:25). From the house of Ham, God chose no one, but from the family of Shem, Noah's son, is descended Abraham, the father of all of the faithful. Now, Abraham already understood the mind of God, for when his son Isaac wished to be married, Abraham told his oldest servant not to take a wife for his son from the daughters of the Canaanites, among whom he dwelt, but to go to his country and to his kindred, and take a wife for his son Isaac [Genesis 24:3,4]. Isaac was of the same mind, because he ordered his son, Jacob, as he blessed him saying: "You shall not marry one of the Canaanite women. Arise, go to . . . the house of . . . your mother's father; and . . . take . . . [a] wife from there . . ." [Genesis 28:1, 2].

But Esau, also a son of Isaac, was an uncouth man and hated God, for he did not respect the mind of God in marrying, but rather followed his own lust and pleasure. He took two women from the Hittites, who were not of his family, and they caused Isaac and Rebekah much grief.

This may be seen in the example of the wise King Solomon when love and lust for foreign women overwhelmed him, and he married contrary to the Law. Thus he fell into the disgrace of God, and finally his entire kingdom was disrupted. Again, it can be seen that when the Jews there were converted, and rebuilt the temple during Nehemiah's time, they had to divorce their foreign wives whom they had married, among whom there were also some with child. This may be read in Ezra, chapter ten.

SON: If people outside of the true faith marry, and one partner is converted and becomes a believer, may he stay with the unbeliever?

FATHER: Indeed, it must have happened often among the early Christians that one partner became a believer and the other did not. Paul teaches that if the unbeliever desires to remain with the believer, the believer should not divorce him. If, however, the unbeliever wishes to be divorced, he may do it, and the believing partner is not bound in such a case (I Corinthians 7:12-15). It is good to note what Paul says in the previous verses about the state of marriage among believers, namely that the Lord says that "the wife should not separate from her husband (but if she does, let her remain single . . .) . . . . To the rest I say, not the Lord, that if any brother has a wife who is an unbeliever, and she consents to live with him, he should not divorce her" [1 Corinthians 7:10-12].

By this we understand that the unbelieving partner must not be a wolf or a brute, as are some men who are like dogs, lions, or wild beasts. They quarrel, blaspheme, and continually try to destroy and ruin with violence all that is good. If the unbeliever were to break out into all kinds of outrage and adultery, so that the believing partner were only a cloak for his scandals, the believer should definitely not be bound to remain with such a vicious person.

[ON ADULTERY]

SON: If then, among married people, one partner were to allow himself to be seduced by the devil to commit adultery, but still wished to remain with the spouse, may this be permitted?

FATHER: In the first place, it is commanded under the Law that adulterers be killed, for there should be none among the people of the Lord. If, however, a man set his wife at liberty by a letter of divorce, she was no adulteress even if she took another husband. However, if the second husband died, the first was not allowed to take her again, because she had become unclean. This was "an abomination before the Lord" (Deuteronomy 24:3, 4).

Now it can easily be seen that if a woman became unclean even if her husband released her by the permissible method, how much more was she unclean if she fell into adultery. How much less then dare a believer, whose body is to be holy, have any further relationship with an adulterous harlots-body? This is certainly a great abomination in the sight of God and can absolutely not be permitted in the church of the Lord. The entire church would be defiled by this. In case such a woman or man truly repented, he or she could continue to live with the innocent partner. However, it would be unclean to have relationships with each other again, according to the pure mind of God.[4]

[ON AVOIDANCE]

SON: If, among believers, one partner sins, be it husband or wife, so that he or she has to be placed in the ban by the church, must then the other partner also avoid the first, and especially in marital relationships?

FATHER: Note here again the plan of God! In the Old Testament, God commanded: "If your brother, the son of your mother, or your son, or your daughter, or the wife of your bosom, or your friend who is as your own soul, entices you secretly, saying 'Let us go and serve other gods,' which neither you nor your father have known, . . . you shall not yield to him or listen to him, nor shall your eye pity him, nor shall you spare him, nor shall you conceal him; but you shall kill him; your hand shall be first against him to put him to death, and afterwards the hand of all the people" (Deuteronomy 13:6-9). You see here that no kinship could help anyone who had to be killed in accordiance with the Law. This prefigured the ban of the church in the New Covenant. The Lord Jesus says that if your brother sins against you (and here is also to be understood husband, wife, child, and parent, if they are united with one another in the covenant of God), and if he refuses to listen to you and the church ". . . let him be to you as a Gentile and a tax collector" (Matthew 18:17).

This is indeed avoidance in spiritual as well as physical relationships. Those persons who are closest to the one banned must justly be the first to avoid him as already mentioned above, if they do not want to be defiled. This is powerfully prefigured in Deuteronomy 17:7; when a person had sinned so that he had to die "the hand of the witnesses shall be first against him to put him to death, and afterward the hand of all the people." When Israel committed sin with the golden calf, according to the Word of the Lord the Levites had to slay in the camp, first, each man's brother, friend, and neighbor, and then the blessing was conferred upon them by Moses.

Therefore, it is the most necessary thing in Christianity to deny the very best for the sake of the Lord. The teachings of Jesus have the same emphasis of self-denial. There are still some unenlightened souls who are willing to help carry out the ban against someone where it requires no self-denial, but if it happens that they themselves, or their dearest friends, or husband, wife, or children should be denied, then, unfortunately, often natural love is much stronger than divine love, and this proves their ruin. There is no eluding this word of the Lord Jesus: "Whoever loves something more than me, he is not worthy of me."

[ON OUTWARD WORSHIP]

SON: You have now told me about various things, but I hear from many that it is not necessary to pay attention to these things, because believers are transformed into heavenly beings and no longer need to trouble themselves with such things.

FATHER: Yes, I have myself seen enough of such men who speak, teach, and write like that. However, they are badly mistaken; they lack humble hearts which gladly submit to divine counsel and ordinances and learn to be faithful in humble tasks. When this is done they will be placed over high and great things. There is a time of humiliation and a time of exaltation. The Lord Jesus first appeared very humbly and lowly in this world in humble and willing submission to the will of His Father. The second time, however, He will appear in great power and glory as an exalted Christ.

All souls who desire to be with Him in His exaltedness must certainly first accept Him as a humble Christ. They must confess Him before men in all of His commandments, and not be ashamed of them. In this way they will become humble in the humble commandments, and then finally they shall be exalted in due season. It will be impossible otherwise.

For this reason, the church of the Lord has always been lowly and despised in this world. It has always been considered as filth [by the unbelieving world]. For this reason those men err badly in their thinking who claim that it is not necessary for believers to be baptized with elementary water; likewise, they do not consider it necessary to drink the common wine of the communion to proclaim the death of Jesus, but rather say that they drink spiritual wine and are baptized with spiritual water, and other similar pretensions contrary to the clear testimony of the Holy Scripture. Therefore, it is very good to look only to the express word of the Lord Jesus and to His own perfect example. If people would just follow after Him in the obedience of faith, taking reason captive in obedience to the Lord Jesus, they would not be led astray by the high-sounding talk of men.

[ON HUMAN TESTIMONY]

SON: I have also heard many who appeal to the saints, such as Tauler, Thomas a Kempis, and others, who have written such beautiful and gifted books but have not recorded anything about observing the outward teachings of Christ.

FATHER: Those persons who appeal to the testimonies of men reveal that they do not possess the divine testimony of Jesus. Therefore Saint John says "If we receive the testimony of men, the testimony of God is greater; for this is the testimony of God that he has borne witness to his Son. He who believes in the Son of God has the testimony in himself. He who does not believe God, has made him a liar, because he has not believed in the testimony that God has borne to his Son" (1 John 5:9, 10). This testimony is necessary for salvation, and all of the saints have had it. It is unfortunately very dangerous to appeal to this testimony of men who have remained within the great Babel. In general, all those who appeal to such men are despite this not in agreement with them. Who, indeed, could be agreed with those who were still in monasteries and under the papal dogma? Perhaps they did not profess what they had actually come to recognize as the truth because of fear of men.

This appealing to holy men is just as blind as the entire world's appealing to Christ and His apostles when it is not one with the latters' lives and teaching. Therefore, those poor souls are indeed to be pitied who wish to build their faith upon such a poor foundation, which always fails when temptation comes. The Son of God taught this: "Every one then who hears these words of mine and does them will be . . . a wise man" (Matthew 7:24). Again, the Savior speaks: "Truly, truly, I say to you, he who hears my word and believes him who sent me, has eternal life; he does not come into judgment . . ." (John 5:24). Again, ". . . whoever lives and believes in me shall never die" [John 11:26].

These are positive testimonies for him who believes. How wretched is it to appeal to testimonies of men and to look to men who are considered holy and wise, so that one is led to think or say: "Truly, if they taught in this way and believed according to the Scriptures, we shall believe it also!" The Apostle Paul speaks against it: "But even if we, or an angel from heaven, should preach to you a gospel contrary to that which we preached to you, let him be accursed" (Galatians 1:8). Behold, this is the only gospel which Moses and all the prophets emphasized that it might be heard, and which was revealed to us by Christ and His apostles. This gospel cannot be altered or violated by the holiness of angels, much less by that of men, or even the might or power of the entire world. They can neither add anything to it nor take anything away, without incurring the great displeasure of God. It stands firm like the mountain of God. It is a stone such as Christ speaks of: "And he who falls on this stone will be broken to pieces; but when it falls on anyone, it will crush him" (Matthew 21:44).

[ON THE REWARD FOR BELIEVERS]

SON: You have told me much about the teaching of Jesus Christ, and that it is necessary to walk according to it under the cross and in trials. What may a man expect if he denies himself and follows Christ, and endures the cross and suffering to the very end?

FATHER: Blessings and glories of such great dignity will be obtained through Christ that no human tongue can express it, nor can be described what God has prepared for those who love Him. Nevertheless, I will tell you as much as has been expressed in the Holy Scriptures by the Spirit of God. The Son of God himself testifies that whoever believes in Him may have eternal life (John 3:15). That is in itself a great pronouncement of eternal glory. This is not the kind of a life that kings and monarchs have in this world, which is scarcely a handsbreadth, and is full of infirmity, illness, fear, unrest, danger of death, and the like and at last is of no avail. Rather, it is a life of joy which is no longer subject to death and remains everlasting. For eternity there is no illness, pain, fear, want, discomfort, war, or disputes; neither weeping nor mourning will be heard.

In the same measure that life will be everlasting, so will joy be everlasting. God spoke this through the prophets: "Everlasting joy [shall be] upon their heads; they shall obtain joy and gladness, and sorrow and sighing shall flee away" (Isaiah 35:10). There will be "the river of the water of life, bright as crystal, flowing from the throne of God and of the Lamb . . .; on either side of the river, the tree of life," bearing the most delicious fruit (Revelation 22:1). In this life of joy, the Holy City of God will reveal itself (Revelation 21). The city and its streets will be of pure gold and precious stones, and the faithful will sing the joyous *Hallelujah* in the streets of the city (Tobit 13:22 [18]). They will wear crowns on their heads, and have palm branches of victory in their hands (Revelation 7). They will sing and make music, and rejoice with great joy. The Lamb will lead them to the spring of the water of life, and they will enjoy the fruits of immortality.

Yes, the joy will always be heightened when they behold the Lord Jesus in His great glory and majesty with His many thousand times a thousand saints and angels who surround His throne and sing *Hallelujah* with holy fervor and joy so that heaven and earth will resound with it. The creatures who have been made free will be led because of this to utter praise, honor, glory and power from eternity to eternity before the strangled Lamb (Revelation 5:15 [13]. More than all this, the greatest delight will be to behold the Lord Jesus in His transfigured humanity. Indeed, they will wonder why so few people loved and followed after Jesus, who alone is all-powerful and glorious.

Yes, the believers will wonder why they were not more willing while in this world, to sacrifice body and soul and all that they had out of love for this heavenly King and His holy teaching. They will realize that the Lord Jesus had left this glory to come to the valley of misery out of love for them—even died out of love for them so that they could obtain this great blessing. This will then move them to give more honor, praise, and gratitude in all eternity.

> Then what a life of jubilee,
> Will there in that period be,
> To the thousands whose happy home,
> Is before, and near to God's throne.
> With rays of glory surrounded,
> With the seraphic host joined

In the heavenly song, thrice holy
Are the Three unit'd in testimony.[5]

[ON PUNISHMENT OF UNBELIEVERS]

SON: If, then, the true and believing soul shall enjoy such great and, indeed, inexpressible blessedness, what will happen to the unbelievers who were not obedient to the commandments of the Lord Jesus, and did not love Him and His Kingdom but rather the world and its glories, and who died in sin?

FATHER: Just as the glories of the believers will be inexpressible, the torment of the condemned and unbelievers will be equally inexpressible. The Scriptures say: "Behold, he is coming with the clouds, and every eye will see him, every one who pierced him; and all tribes of the earth will wail on account of him" (Revelation 1:7). They will cry to the mountains and hills in sheer fear and terror: "Fall on us and hide us from the face of him who is seated on the throne, and from the wrath of the Lamb" (Revelation 6:16). That will no longer help them, for they will have to listen as Christ says: "Depart from me, you cursed, into the eternal fire prepared for the devil and his angels . . ." (Matthew 25 [:41]). "If any one worships the beast and its image . . . he shall be tormented with fire and brimstone in the presence of the holy angels and in the presence of the Lamb. And the smoke of their torment goes up for ever and ever; and they have no rest, day or night . . ." (Revelation 14:[9] 10, 11).

If anyone's name is not found in the Book of Life, he will be thrown into the lake of fire, where the worm does not die and the fire will not be quenched (Revelation 20:15; Mark 9:48; Isaiah 66:24). They will be an abomination to all flesh. In all of their torment, the pain will be increased the more when they realize how they frivolously forfeited through folly the great blessedness and glories which they now see in the children of God, when they still lived in the time of grace. They did not respect them then, but heedlessly spent the time in every sin. Then the righteous will stand with great gladness opposite those who had so persecuted them and rejected their work (their teaching and faith in Jesus Christ). Then the damned will see this and stand in dreadful awe of such blessedness, and will say to one another with penitence, and sigh with anguish of the spirit: " This is the man we fools once laughed at . . .. We thought his life was madness . . .. How did he come to be reckoned among the sons of God, and why is his lot among the saints? Then we must have wandered from the true way . . .. What good did our arrogance do us? And what have wealth and ostentation done for us?" (Wisdom of Solomon 5:1 [4-8]).

They will ponder all of these things—how they spent their lives in sin, how they did not love God as the highest good, and lost through this folly all this great blessedness. Then they will experience torment, grief, and misery which no tongue can express, for they are banished from the presence of God and all the saints.

[ON UNIVERSAL RESTORATION]

SON: These things are most horrible to hear. Do tell me are these torments and tortures to last for eternity, without end?

FATHER: According to the testimony of the Holy Scriptures, "the smoke of their torment goes up forever and ever" (Revelation 14:11). However, that it should last for eternity is not supported by Holy Scriptures. It is not necessary to talk much about it or speculate about it. The joyous blessedness is definitely forfeited by their folly. Even if at some time the torment should end after long eternities, they will never attain that which the believers have achieved in the time of grace through Jesus Christ if they obey Him. Many who have heard about universal restoration commit the great folly not to deny themselves completely but rather hope for the restoration. This hope will most certainly come to naught when they enter the torment, and can see no end to it. Their pitiful comfort will vanish like smoke.

Therefore, it is much better to practice this simple truth that one should try to become worthy in the time of grace to escape the wrath of God and the torments of hell, rather than deliberate how or when it would be possible to escape from it again. It is as if a thief were to console himself like this: "Oh, even if I am seized because of the theft, my punishment will have its end." Would not that be a miserable consolation! Therefore, that is a much better and more blessed gospel which teaches how to escape the wrath of God than the gospel which teaches that eternal punishment has an end. Even though this is true, it should not be preached as a gospel to the godless. Unfortunately, in this day, everything is completely distorted by the great power of imagination of those people who teach and write books about restoration.

[ON SPIRITUAL FOOD]

There are very few faithful stewards who were established by the Lord Jesus over His house who "give them their portion of food at the proper time" (Luke 12:42). Give children milk, youths more nourishing food, and to the mature the most solid food. But there are so many unfaithful stewards who were not set over the servants of the house by the Lord himself, but run according to their own pleasures by human wisdom. They wish to be clever people, but they distort the plan and intent of the Lord. They give solid food to those to whom they should give milk. Of this, the Apostle Paul said at Corinth: "I fed you with milk, not solid food, for you were not ready for it . . .; you are still of the flesh" (1 Corinthians 3:1, 2).

The same is true in the spiritual as in the natural life. If milk were to be withheld from a young infant, and it were given instead a delicious roast, one would certainly find out that the child would soon die, even though the meat itself was very good and delicious. The same happens, unfortunately, also in these troubled times, when many souls have been awakened by grace to repentance, and are still young children in the faith. They should rightly be given the first principles of the Christian life—the proper milk-food, as Peter points out (1 Peter 2[:2]), that they should grow up as do the newborn babies. However, this pure milk is withdrawn from them by making them suspicious of it, and by presenting them with more solid food.

The consequences of this cannot be enough lamented, because they result in nothing but harm, death and ruin, distraction and division. When such a teacher and steward has presented solid food for a long time, he departs again, and the poor people do not know what it really was. It is true, they were long led by a beautiful sound, but it was an indistinct tone. Therefore, no one has been able to prepare himself properly for the strife against the devil and his following. Paul compares such people to a "noisy gong or a clanging cymbal" (1 Corinthians 13:1), because they do not have the teaching and love, through which the ordinances and commandment of God can be kept (John 14; 1 John 5:3).

[CONCLUSION: FATHERLY ADVICE]

SON: Dear father, I thank you again for your good instructions. Because this journey is just about over, I would like to ask yet this question: I have well understood from you, and also believe, that the way to life is very narrow and straight, and the deception of the work is great, there being so many false spirits, false teachers, amd false prophets. How should I conduct myself in these times so that I might obtain eternal salvation, and avoid being misled?

FATHER: I will give you good and sure counsel out of fatherly love. Bear this in mind all your life; never let it escape your heart, but remember it wherever you go and are—when you lie down and when you rise. Let this be your greatest concern that all of your sighs and desires be directed toward loving your God (who has created you) and toward loving Jesus Christ (who has redeemed you with His precious blood) with all your heart, all your soul, and all your mind above all things of the world, be it beauty or wealth, yes, whatever may come within your sight or your hearing.

Fear God in this love with a childlike heart, contemplate all of His commandments day and night, keep them with a pure heart, let them be your counselors, and pray unceasingly for the Holy Spirit, who will guide you in truth in all of the commandments of God. Let continually ring in your ears that which David says: "How can a young man keep his way pure? By guarding it according to thy word" (Psalm 119:9). Again, "The promises of the Lord are promises that are pure, silver refined in a furnace on the ground, purified seven times" (Psalm 12:7[6]). Further, "The law of the Lord is perfect, reviving the soul; the testimony of the Lord is sure, making wise the simple; the precepts of the Lord are right, rejoicing the heart; the commandment of the Lord is pure, enlightening the eyes . . .. More to be desired are they than gold, even much fine gold; sweeter also than honey and drippings of the honeycomb" (Psalm 19:8, 11 [7, 8, 10]).

Moreover, let continually resound in your mind the words of the Lord Jesus: "If a man loves me, he will keep my word . . . . He who does not love me does not keep my words" (John 14:23, 24). Again, "My sheep hear my voice, and I know them, and they follow me; and I give them eternal life" (John

10:27 [and 28]). Besides this always remember in your heart what the Lord Jesus says about His commandments when He speaks: " For I have not spoken on my own authority; the Father who sent me has himself given me commandment what to say and what to speak" (John 12:49, 50). Always keep the dear counsel of the Lord Jesus, which He gives to His own, when He says: "Beware of false prophets, who come to you in sheep's clothing but inwardly are ravenous wolves" (Matthew 7:15). Further: "Take heed, that no one lead you astray. For many will come in my name, saying, 'I am the Christ,' and they will lead many astray" (Matthew 24:4, 5).

Always bear your soul in your hands as your most precious treasure, and walk in holy fear at all times. Speak with David with a pure heart to God: "With regard to the works of men, by the word of thy lips I have avoided the ways of the violent" (Psalm 17:4). You may encounter such men and be in the company of those who seem to you much more holy than John, more zealous than Elijah, more miracle-working than Moses, and appearing more humble and spiritually minded than Christ himself or His apostles. If they do not walk in the teachings of Jesus the crucified Savior, as written in the New Testament, and they wish to lead you away from these simple commandments of the Lord Jesus, remember this and believe it in your heart—they are false apostles and deceitful workers. Close your eyes to their gospel, be wise as a serpent which stops its ears to the charmer, and call and cry to Jesus as a sheep to its shepherd.

SON: I must ask you yet something else. It seems to me somewhat harsh that I should consider those men false prophets who prove themselves with such sanctity and gift of working miracles, even if they do not walk in the ways of the Lord and are opposed to what is written outwardly in the [New] Testament.

FATHER: I should have thought that you would have well understood the divine plan after this long conversation. I will repeat it in accordance with the testimony of the Holy Scriptures, of both Old and New Testaments. When God revealed His Law to the people of Israel through Moses, it was a definite rule that whoever broke the Law of Moses must die (Numbers 15:35; Hebrews 10:28). But the person who did anything with a high hand reviled the Lord, and that person was cut off from among the people and his iniquity was upon him. So strict was the word of the Lord given through Moses!

Now, all those who added to or took away from the Law were false prophets. The true prophets all adhered to and observed the Law, as the servant Moses had spoken it. The false one walked according to their hearts' desires but did say to the people, "Thus spoke the Lord." But these were only lies. Now, notice well what kind of teaching, statutes, and laws were introduced by the Son of God himself, and were confirmed by "signs and wonders and various miracles and by gifts of the Holy Spirit distributed according to His own will" (Hebrews 2:4) by the Son of God, through whom the Father has spoken to us "in these last days" (Hebrews 1:1, 2)—by whom the Father "made the whole world"; who is that living "Word become flesh" (John 1[:14]); to whom the Father has given "all authority in heaven and on earth" (Matthew 28:18); which law is "far above all rule and authority and power and dominion . . . not only in this age but also in that which is to come" (Ephesians 1:21). It is the Son of God who "has gone into heaven and is at the right hand of God, with angels, authorities, and powers subject to him" (1 Peter 3:22).

Now, consider how much better the teaching of the Son of God must be kept, how much more strictly and unfalteringly, by all those who believe in His teachings, commandments, good counsel, and laws. From this you can easily determine how wicked, how arrogant, how blind, and how dark a soul must be to despise a single command of the Lord Jesus. How much more wicked must those teachers and prophets be who despise in their wisdom the wisdom of Jesus and wish to make a different path from that which Jesus ordained. They seek to mislead those souls who wish to follow Jesus in His commands in a simple way—some try it through eloquent speeches, disguised in sheep's clothing; others threaten with imprisonment and seek to prevent these souls from the good counsel of Jesus by threats and all kinds of persecution.

What do you think? Are they not the deceivers, false prophets, yes, thieves and murderers, who have always tried to climb over the wall, and will not enter by the door—which is Jesus himself (John 10 [:1, 2]). There is nothing more abominable and more sinful in the sight of God than when a mortal man does not believe His God in all His commands and prohibitions. You will not find another salvation in the Old and New Testaments outside of this, except only that the will of God has been the salvation of the souls, and will always remain so.

This is the way to God if a soul does that which is agreeable to the will of God. If he does not do it and opposes himself to his God with his will because of deprecating Him, thinking and speaking that certain things are not necessary for him although God has commanded them—then this soul is an enemy of God. Saint John says: "Any one who goes ahead and does not abide in the doctrine of Christ does not have God" (2 John, verse 9). Whoever remains in the teaching of Christ has both Father and Son. Therefore, I will advise you this, in conclusion, that you should look alone to Jesus your Redeemer and Savior (Hebrews 12:2). If you have learned from Him the teaching as it is outwardly commanded in the Testament, so that you will remain steadfast in it, and resolve yourself to sacrifice your life, your property, family, yes, all that you have in the whole world—rather than waver from His teaching—you must become used to taking His cross upon yourself daily with denial of your will. Otherwise, you cannot be a disciple of the Lord Jesus, much less an heir of His Kingdom (Luke 14:27).

Now, may the Lord Jesus bless our soul, and strengthen your faith, and let his simple instruction grow within you and bear fruit which will remain for life eternal. We will together praise and glorify our God forever. Amen.

The Sin-Expunging Jesus
(Der Sunden austilgende Jesus)

A pard'ning Lord I am,
In love I will be found.
The Son of God and man,
To heal the sinful wound.
All is now gained,
My death has bought,
And pardon wrought
That you be spared.

Your sin I cast away,
It shall return no more;
Your debt I had to pay,
And suffered for it sore.
My blood I gave,
My life I spent,
Through death I went
For you to save.

This have I done for you;
Be faithful then, and true;
Do not depart from me,
I shall be faithful too.
Then watch and pray,
And love me too,
Who first loved you
And am your stay.[6]

Translator's footnotes:

1. Later editions add: ". . . by Jeremias Felbinger."

2. The preceding two paragraphs are omitted in later editions.

3. This obviously incorrect quotation may have been taken from a sixteenth-century statement against infant baptism. The following passage, found in the writing of an Anabaptist martyr, Thomas Imbroich (1533-1558), was reprinted in the eighteenth century by the Mennonites: ". . . thus says Tertullian (in his book *On the Chaplet*): 'Those who are to be baptized profess there, and also some time previously in the church before the bishop that they renounce the devil, his pomp and angels; after this they are immersed three times and baptized.' Renan notes at this passage that the old custom was that the adults were baptized and washed with the bath of rebirth, [and that] this custom was maintained until the time of Charles the Great, Ludovici the emperor, in the year 801; Ludovicus became emperor in the year 815 after Christ's birth." —'Widerspruch von einem, der sich nennet *Petrus* (und sein Gegentheil *Thomas*). Welcher die Kinder-Tauffle ohne Grund und Zeugnisz heiliger Schrifft wil erhalten und bewahren,' in *Confessio Pulchra* . . . , part of *Guldene Aepffel in Silbern Schalen* . . . (Ephrata, Pennsylvania: the Community, 1745), page 74; first printed in Europe in 1702.]

4. In some English versions, Matthew 18:8, 9 is here inserted.

5. From the Kurtz translation.

6. Once presumed to have been written by Alexander Mack, it is now known that this hymn was written by Joachim Neander. This is largely Kurtz' translation.

Count Well the Cost

MACH'S MIT MIR, GOTT. 8 7 8 7 8 8

Alexander Mack, Sr., 1679-1735
Tr. by Ora W. Garber, b. 1903

Johann Hermann Schein, 1586-1630
Harm. by J. S. Bach, 1685-1750

1. Christ Je - sus says, "Count well the cost When you lay the foun - da - tion." Are you re - solved, though all seem lost, To risk your rep - u - ta - tion, Your self, your wealth, for Christ the Lord As you now give your sol - emn word?

2. With - in the church's warm em - brace The child of God is mold - ed, God's Spir - it light - ing up his face And by His grace en - fold - ed. His child - like steps trace out Christ's plan And he be - comes a god - ly man.

3. With - in the church's shel - tering fold God is His truth re - veal - ing. Thro' Christ, His Son, all men are told To heed His warm ap - peal - ing; For all the truth through Him made known Is sealed with blood that is His own.

4. Up, sons of men! The time is right To ward off ills im - pend - ing, For Christ Him - self joins in the fight, His right - eous realm de - fend - ing. To do this, have the mind of Christ; His Word at all times has suf - ficed. A-MEN.

Mack's hymn, Count the Cost, translated by Ora Garber
and set to the music of Schein (Bach).

Count the Cost

The first Brethren hymnal, the *Geistreiches Gesang=Buch*, was printed in Berleburg in 1720. Of the 295 hymns, about 100 were written by the early Brethren. One, *Count the Cost*, seems clearly to have been authored by Alexander Mack. It is said to have been sung by the members during baptismal services. It is presented here in two translations. The one by Ora W. Garber is intended to be sung and has, in fact, been set to a tune by Schein and Bach from that period. The second translation, by Hedda Durnbaugh, is a more literal, prose translation. She describes this as a "teaching hymn, in which . . . Alexander Mack explains the meaning of baptism, compares the church to the vine, gives a brief sketch of God's plan for the restoration of humankind, adds some sound Christian advice, and concludes with a call to action against the evils of the times."

A. Count Well the Cost

1

Christ Jesus says, "Count well the cost
When you lay the foundation."
Are you resolved, though all seem lost,
To risk your reputation,
Your self, your wealth, for Christ the Lord
As you now give your solemn word?

2

Into Christ's death you're buried now
Through baptism's joyous union.
No claim of self dare you allow
If you desire communion
With Christ's true church, His willing bride,
Which, through His Word, He has supplied.

3

When from the heart all sin you loathe,
Then you will be succeeding
Yourself with righteousness to clothe.
The struggle still proceeding,
Your righteousness can hold at bay
This world's false god, athwart your way.

4

Within the church's warm embrace
The child of God is molded,
God's Spirit lighting up his face
And by His grace enfolded.
His childlike steps trace out Christ's plan
And he becomes a godly man.

5

In Christian growth he is matured,
Of fruitful vines a token.
That this good growth may be assured,
Ofttimes to him is broken
The bread of fellowship replete
When Christ's redeemed together meet.

6

Within the church's sheltering fold
God is His truth revealing;
Through Christ, His Son, all men are told
To heed His warm appealing,
For all the truth through Him made known
Is sealed with blood that is His own.

7

His testimony is as true
As when the church received it
Long years ago, while it was new,
And with glad hearts believed it.
Through signs that dare not be denied,
The new has pushed the old aside.

8

By means of wonder and of sign
God brought the old to being.
As later years brought its decline

There was no need of seeing.
When Joshua had heard it read,
His faith required no sign, he said.

9

He who has faith in God's sure Word
Will not demand a token.
When Christ rebuked the evil horde,
Their unbelief plain spoken,
He showed a sign, at their request,
But they remained quite unimpressed.

10

Consider well what Abraham said
When the rich man suggested,
From that realm of the tortured dead,
That Lazarus be requested
To warn his brothers of hell's pain
While in this world they yet remain.

11

That boon by Abraham was denied.
From all that is deceiving
The heart must be made right inside
Ere there can be believing;
The Law and the prophetic Word
Project faith's light upon our Lord.

12

Against false teaching guard your heart.
Some practice at deceiving
And make it seem, by sinful art,
As if to Christ they're cleaving.
If from Christ's Word one does not teach,
His words are but deceptive speech.

13

Up, sons of men! The time is right
To ward off ills impending,
For Christ himself joins in the fight,
His righteous realm defending.
To do this, have the mind of Christ;
His Word at all times has sufficed.

—Translated By Ora W. Garber

B. Count the Cost

1

"Count the cost," says Jesus Christ, when you will lay the foundation. Are you willing, in your own mind, to risk your wealth, body, possessions, and your honor, in following Christ's example, as you are about to promise?

2

Through baptism you are buried into Christ's death and will no longer be allowed to be your own, if you are minded to be co-inheritor with Christ's church [*Gemeinde*] and his bride, whom he has created through his word.

3

If you hate sin from the bottom of your heart, you will succeed; gird yourself with righteousness and you will be able to do battle with your enemy, the god of the world, who is obstructing your path.

4

The child is formed in the bosom of the church according to the Father's will. His spirit fills it and removed the [old] garments, the childish indecision disappears, and the child becomes an adult according to Christ's mind.

5

This adult is incorporated [into the church] to grow into a fruitful vine. To this end he will often be offered the bread of fellowship when the church gathers who are Christ's body and members.

6

They are truly in the house of God where God teaches them through his son, of whom it is said that one should listen to him in all that he teaches which is sealed through his own blood.

7

His testament is still as valid as it was a thousand years ago with the disciples to whom God had revealed it through sign, miracles, and through power, through which the old was abolished.

8

When later on it was destroyed, there was no evidence of any sign anymore. When Joshua heard it read, he believed and no longer asked for a sign.

9

Whoever believes in the word of God will not demand a sign, for Christ reprimanded the evil band whose unbelief became manifest when they demanded a sign. When he did acceed, they did not believe it.

10

O dear soul [*Mensch*], remember the words which Abraham said to the rich man who, after he had died, asked Lazarus to tell his brothers about the agony and pain that they might believe it.

11

Abraham denied him this, he took it as unbelief. Their hearts had to be directed towards faith in God and his word, as the writings of Moses and the prophets directed towards Christ, the light.

12

Keep your heart from false teachings and do not be deceived by those who pretend that they, too, listen to Christ. If someone does not follow Christ's word in his own teaching, then what such a person says is not true.

13

Arise, dear soul[*Menschen-Kind*], the time is now to stem the evil, for Christ himself goes into battle against those who will not listen to him in his outer and inner word. But those who do, have the mind of Christ.

—Translated by Hedda T. Durnbaugh

Miscellaneous Notes

The following notes appear in the personal Bible of Alexander Mack, Sr., which has been preserved in the Mack Library at Bridgewater College in Virginia. Some of these notes were first published by Henry Kurtz in an early issue of the Gospel Visitor (1852). This translation is by Donald Durnbaugh from his book, *The Brethren in Colonial America* (p. 426-428).

The first operation of grace in the soul is a true awakening from the carefree slumber in sin and separation from God, and a recognition of our poverty and revelation of the divine life. Out of this arises in the soul the hunger and desire for help, sanctification, forgiveness of sins, and righteousness. Then grace shows how sanctification and forgiveness, indeed everything, can be received from Jesus alone. Then grace effects obedience to Jesus and, prior to this, the true faith out of which obedience issues.

. . . . .

The following passages demonstrate to us the kind of tongues of the old man of sin: Sirach, chapter 28; Psalms 5 and 140; James 3; Proverbs 18.

Now follow the passages which demonstate the manner of new tongues of the newborn children and heirs of the kingdom: Proverbs, chapters 12 and 15; Song of Solomon 4; Isaih 35 and 52; Acts 2, 10, and 19; Zephaniah 3:13; Revelation 14.

. . . . .

St. Dionysius was a bishop of Ascalon in the Holy Land, and at his time it was said that Clement asserted that the Lord Jesus had baptized the apostle Peter, and Peter had baptized James and John and Andrew, and these in turn had baptized all [the] apostles (page 755 in the book called "The First Temple of God in Christ").

· · · · ·

It is Almighty God who created all nature, human beings as well as beasts, and when nature suffers want, God, its Creator, has mercy and comes to its assistance. Therefore David says that the Lord gives to the beast his food and to the young ravens which cry. Yes, in Psalm 104[:27] David says: "These all look to thee, to give them their food in due season. When thou givest to them, they gather it up; when thou openest thy hand, they are filled with good things. When thou hidest thy face, they are dismayed; when thou takest away their breath, they die and return to their dust." Oh, wonderful, eternal, and almighty Creator and Sustainer of all angels, men, and all creatures! Hallelujah!

· · · · ·

In the Book of Concord of the Augsburg Confession, printed in 1580, page 221, there is said to be a reference to more than seven thousand Lutheran theologians who speak about immersion baptism as follows [in Dutch]: That they immerse us in the water which closes in above us, and then pull us out again; this immersing and pulling out again makes up the power of baptism. Also, Zwingli in his book written against the Catabaptists, page 17, states that the Zurich authorities ordered that whoever was or would be baptized by immersion was to be drowned by immersion. This was directed against the Anabaptists.

· · · · ·

A scholar named Coccejus thoroughly discusses in his *Thesaurus Catolica,* volume 2, book 5, article 16, that no other baptism was generally practiced in the church from 100 A.D. until 1600 A.D. than immersion baptism, that thus sprinking also of children, did not become completely predominant before the year 1600, even though it had already begun with Luther. However, Luther himself wrote sharply against this [practice]. Indeed, in the entire Russian empire to this day they still baptize children by immersion and consider sprinkling not a valid form of baptism because they belong to the Greek [Orthodox] Church.

. . . . .

The learned astronomers write that the sun is 166 times larger than the entire earth and that the sun is 187,000 miles in distance above the earth and that the planet Mercury is twenty-two times larger than the earth and is seven thousand miles in distance above the earth. The planet Jupiter is ninety-five times larger than the earth and is many thousands of miles in distance above the earth. Oh, what a wonderfully great and incomprehensible Creator must He be who has created and sustained such creations!

God has thus placed man in this world as in a foreign garden, in which he is to live and eat of all its fruits, but he is not allowed to take anything away with him. Rather, he must leave everything in the world just as God commanded in the law in the book of Deuteronomy, chapter 23[:24]: "When you go into your neighbor's vineyard, you may eat your fill of grapes, as many as you wish, but you shall not put any in your vessel" to carry out. It is the same with the riches of this world, with eating, drinking and clothing. But when man wants or has to leave [the world] again, he is not allowed to take anything along even if he had been a king. That is why Jesus teaches the renunciation of the riches of this world, even of one's life. Has it not been very wonderfully and wisely ordained by God that men have the best things in common such as life and body? Now Jesus says that life is more than eating and the body is more than clothing. Thus the wealthiest people in this world have a small advantage only in the lowliest things, such as in food and clothing.

BIBLIOGRAPHY

A. Published Editions of Mack's Writings

1. Grundforschende Fragen von der Wassertaufe. July, 1713. Berleburg? Christoph Konnert? No copy of original known. Title taken from Jacob Haug's Catalogus Librorum (Berleburg, 1729). Hereafter referred to as Grundforschende Fragen.

2. Kurtze und einfaltige Vorstellung, Der auszeren aber doch heiligen Rechten und Ordnungen desz Hauses Gottes. 1715. Probably at Berleburg by Konnert. 94 pp. Hereafter referred to as Rechten und Ordnungen.

3. Ueberschlag die Kost. In: Geistreiches Gesang-Buch, pp. 7-9. Berleburg, Christoph Konnert, 1720. Original printing of Mack's hymn, Count the Cost.

4. Grundforschende Fragen. Germantown, Christoph Sauer, 1744. 58 pp. Bound and published with No. 5. Second edition and first American printing.

5. Rechten und Ordnungen. Germantown, Christoph Sauer, 1744. 134 pp. Bound and published with No. 4. Second edition and first American printing.

6. Grundforschende Fragen. In: *Christliches Hand-Buchlein . . .* von Jeremias Felbinger. Baltimore, Samuel Sauer, 1799. 41 pp. Bound and published with No. 7. Third edition.

7. Rechten und Ordnungen. In: *Christliches Hand-Buchlein . . .* von Jeremias Felbinger. Baltimore, Samuel Sauer, 1799. 100 pp. Bound and published with No. 6. Third edition.

8. A Short and Plain View of the Outward, Yet Sacred Rights and Ordinances of the House of God. Philadelphia, John Binns, 1810. pp. 1-106. First English translation of Rechten und Ordnungen. Hereafter referred to as Rights and Ordinances. Published with No. 9.

9. Groundsearching Questions. Philadelphia, John Binns, 1810. pp. 106-133. First English translation of Grundforschende Fragen. Hereafter referred to as Groundsearching (or Basic) Questions. Published with No. 8.

10. Grundforschende Fragen. Lancaster, Pa., Johann Bar, 1822. A reprinting of No. 6.

11. Rechten und Ordnungen. Lancaster, Pa., Johann Bar, 1822. A reprinting of No. 7.

12. Groundsearching Questions. In: GOSPEL VISITOR, Vol. IV, pp. 20-23; 37-43; 61-65; 136-139. Poland, Ohio, by Henry Kurtz, 1854. A translation by Kurtz of No. 10. An alert reader provided the editor the missing question 40, which he included both in German and English (pp. 137-138).

13. Rights and Ordinances. In: GOSPEL VISITOR, Vol. V, pp. 144-148; 171-176; 189-191. Poland, Ohio, by Henry Kurtz, 1854. A translation by Kurtz of No. 11. A partial printing of this larger work.

14. Rechten und Ordnungen. Columbiana, Ohio, by Henry Kurtz. pp. 29-110. Parallel German and English columns. Published with No. 16 and 17. 1860.

15. Rights and Ordinances. Columbiana, Ohio, by Henry Kurtz. pp. 29-110. Parallel German and English columns. Published with No. 16 and 17. 1860.

16. Grundforschende Fragen. Columbiana, Ohio, by Henry Kurtz. pp. 113-140. Parallel German and English columns. Published with No. 14 and 15. 1860.

17. Groundsearching Questions. Columbiana, Ohio, by Henry Kurtz. pp. 113-140. Parallel German and English columns. Published with No. 14 and 15. 1860.

18, 19, 20, and 21. The above nos. 14-17 were included by Henry Kurtz in an exact reprinting in The Brethren's Encyclopedia, published at Columbiana, Ohio, in 1867.

22. Rites (sic) and Ordinances. Mount Morris, Ill, The Brethren's Publishing Company, 1888. pp. 13-71. A reprinting of No. 15. Published with No. 23.

23. Ground-Searching Questions. Mount Morris, Ill, The Brethren's Publishing Company, 1888. pp. 72-89. A reprinting of No. 17. Published with No. 22.

24. Groundsearching Questions. In: Holsinger's *History of the Tunkers and the Brethren Church*, pp. 52-73. Lathrop, California, by H. R. Holsinger, 1901.

25. Rights and Ordinances (A Conversation Between Father and Son). In: Holsinger's *History of the Tunkers and the Brethren Church*, pp. 73-117. Lathrop, California, by H. R. Holsinger, 1901. An abridged version, omitting the questions of the son and including only Mack's answers.

26. Groundsearching Questions. In: Early Church History from able and worthy writer concerning Primitive Christianity, compiled by the authority of the "Old Brethren" Yearly Meeting held at Rossville, Indiana, May 27, 1917. pp 33-70. Goshen, Ind., for the Old Brethren Yearly Meeting, 1919.

27. Rites (sic) and Ordinances. Ashland, Ohio, for the National Sunday School Association of the Brethren Church, 1939. pp. 18-73. Published with No. 28.

28. Ground-Searching Questions. Ashland, Ohio, for the National Sunday School Association of the Brethren Church, 1939. pp. 75-93. Published with No. 27.

29. Rites (sic) and Ordinances. Taneytown, Maryland, for the Dunkard Church. 1954. pp. 18-69. Published with No. 30.

30. Ground Searching Questions. Taneytown, Maryland, for the Dunkard Church. 1954. pp. 70-87. Published with No. 29.

31. Basic Questions. In: *European Origins of the Brethren*, by Donald Durnbaugh, pp. 325-344. Elgin, Ill., 1958. A new translation by Donald Durnbaugh.

32. Rights and Ordinances. In: *European Origins of the Brethren*, by Donald Durnbaugh, pp. 344-405. Elgin, Ill., 1958. A new translation by Donald Durnbaugh.

33. Count Well the Cost. In: *European Origins of the Brethren*, by Donald Durnbaugh, pp. 408-411. Elgin, Ill., 1958. A translation of No. 3 by Ora W. Garber; all 13 verses.

34. Count Well the Cost. In: Anniversary Hymns (4 pp.). Elgin, Ill, 1958. Translation by Ora W. Garber; 4 verses with notation.

35. Rites (sic) and Ordinances. In: *Christian Handbook* by J. Felbinger, pp. 1-73. Dayton, Ohio, by J. W. Miller, 1975. A reprint of No. 27.

36. Ground-Searching Questions. In: *Christian Handbook* by J. Felbinger, pp. 76-93. Dayton, Ohio, by J. W. Miller, 1975. A reprint of No. 28.

37. Count the Cost. In: *The German Hymnody of the Brethren 1720-1903*, by Hedwig T. Durnbaugh, pp. 20-21. Philadelphia, The Brethren Encyclopedia, Inc., 1986. A new translation of No. 3 by Hedda Durnbaugh.

B. Important References for the Study of Mack's Writings

1. Durnbaugh, Donald F. 1958. *European Origins of the Brethren*. The Brethren Press, Elgin, Ill. Primary source of most of the translations used in the present volume.

2. Durnbaugh, Donald F. 1960. *Brethren Beginnings: The Origins of the Church of the Brethren in Early Eighteenth-Century Europe*. A dissertation presented to the Graduate School of Arts and Sciences of the University of Pennsylvania. Important comments on portions of the writings of Mack.

3. Durnbaugh, Donald F. 1967. *The Brethren in Colonial America*. The Brethren Press, Elgin, Ill. A new translation of the writings in Mack's Bible, now preserved at Bridgewater College.

4. Durnbaugh, Donald F., editor. 1983. *The Brethren Encyclopedia*, 3 volumes. Brethren Encyclopedia, Inc., Philadelphia, PA and Oak Brook, Ill. Many pertinent articles and important bibliographic details.

5. Durnbaugh, Hedwig T. 1986. *The German Hymnody of the Brethren 1720-1903*. Brethren Encyclopedia Monograph Series No. 1. Brethren Encyclopedia, Inc., Philadephia, PA. Important hymnological treatment of the first Brethren hymnal and analysis of Mack's hymn, Count the Cost.

6. Hinks, Donald R. 1986. *Brethren Hymn Books and Hymnals 1720-1884*. Brethren Heritage Press, Gettysburg, PA. Important bibliographic study of early Brethren hymnals (see pp. 13-21 for the first hymnbook published in Germany.)

7. Stoffer, Dale R. 1989. *Background and Development of Brethren Doctrines 1650-1987*. Brethren Encyclopedia Monograph Series No. 2. Brethren Encyclopedia, Inc., Philadelphia, PA. Important theological analysis of Mack's writings, especially pp. 65-86.

8. Willoughby, William G. 1979. *Counting the Cost*. The Brethren Press, Elgin, Ill. The standard biography of Alexander Mack.